Awakening to Angels

A Study of Angels

BRENDA K. FIELDS

Awakening to Angels

Copyright © 2017 by Brenda K. Fields

All rights reserved. Printed in the United States of America. No part of this publication may be reproduced, stored in a retrieval system, or transmitted, in any form or by any means electronic, mechanical, photocopying, recording, or otherwise, without the prior written permission of the author except in the case of brief quotations embodied in critical articles and reviews.

ISBN: 978-1-942814-01-6

Cover Design: Donna Osborn Clark at www.CreationByDonna.com

Layout and Interior Design: CreationsByDonna@gmail.com

Editing: Shell Vera at www.eyesstraightahead.com

Published by: Kingdom Connection Publications

For information on booking or to contact the Author:
Email: AuthorBrendaFields@gmail.com
Facebook: Author Brenda Fields
Fax: 1-866-823-5529

This book is dedicated to:

My Lord and personal Savior Jesus Christ for selecting me to write this book and share with the world what the Word of God teaches concerning His angels and how we can lose them into our lives.

My parents, The Late Elder Eugene and Mrs. Beulah Fields, for introducing me to Jesus Christ.

Thank You

I extend a special thank you to the following people for your contributions to this book and for allowing me to share your angelic encounters with the world:

My Special Friend, Mrs. Lucille Allen of Montgomery, Alabama

Mr. John W. Barfield, founder of The Bartech Group Inc.; Author of *Starting from Scratch: The Humble Beginnings of a Two-Billion Dollar Enterprise*; Ypsilanti, Michigan

Prophet Nathan Irving, Intercessory Missionary; International Worship Leader; Fredericksburg, Maryland

Apostle Axel Sippach, Apostle to the Nations; Founder and Presiding Apostle of EPIC Global Network (E7); Seattle, Washington

Minister Marcus Stanley, Musician and Producer of *The Marcus Stanley Project* and *An Instrument of Praise;* Richmond, Virginia

Pastor Donnie Williams, II, Pastor and Founder of The Miracle Center International Ministry; Author of *Whatsoever You Do Will Prosper: A Guide for Miraculous Prayer*; Catonsville, Maryland

Foreword

Imagine living a life with the greatest confidence in truly knowing, embracing, and fulfilling this absolute truth: that absolutely no weapon that is formed against you will prosper (Isaiah 54:17, emphasis added). **Do you realize what this means?**

One morning, you could wake up and complete your morning regimen of drinking your coffee, milk, orange juice, and/or tea; eat your typical breakfast; shower; get dressed; read and/or view the morning news; take your children to school; say "I love you" to your husband or wife and your children; and then drive to your workplace like every other morning. Except this morning, out of nowhere, the driver of an 18-wheeler loses control and you become stuck in a car with no way to escape; yet, you are rescued by the fire responders with only a few scratches on your face and arms.

Understandably, you are hysterical and stunned because what just happened to you could be deemed a fatal accident had circumstances differed. As you look at your vehicle while the paramedics are catering to your body, vital signs, blood pressure, etc., you notice that your vehicle is totally crushed. When you reflect on the totaled vehicle and the impact of the collision, you realize that you've just survived a fatal car accident. Miraculously, all you have to show, as proof to your supervisor, to explain why you missed work are a few scratches on your arms and face.

As you tell your friends, family, and colleagues what happened, you value and understand the importance of God's plan for your life each time you say, "There was no rational way in the world that I should have survived that car accident! It should have been fatal!" In fact, the most impeccable words you hold onto are, "There was no way…."

Do you realize that, our lives can be snatched away in less than a second or within a blink of an eye at any time or place, and under any circumstance?

The United States Government's Executive Branch understands that there are threats against the lives of its constituents. Therefore, they have the best-trained men and women to protect some of the most important people to the world. Because our government understands the dire need to have high profile governmental officials, such as the President of the United States, the most secure protection is given to these men and women.

There are many levels of protection every citizen receives in the United States: the neighborhood and community patrol; contracted store security guards; local and state police; and military regimes such as the National Guard, the CIA, NSA, and FBI. Of all the power and authority these protective branches have, even the highest branches of protection cannot do what God's angels can do. After reading Awakening to Angels, you will understand that you have the most powerful army fighting, protecting, and warring on your behalf, as well as completing other assignments.

I wholeheartedly believe that Jesus' love for humanity is so great that He desires for us to fulfill His purposes on Earth before we die. Unfortunately, some do not fulfill the purposes of God because life goes by quickly and they assumed they had more time. Because God is jealous for us, He believes that humanity is so important that even the CIA is not fully equipped to protect us from threatened attacks that are planned against us in the spirit realm. For this reason, He provided us with angels.

Brenda Fields is a Bible scholar who has studied and learned about angels from a Biblical perspective. The Lord has raised her up to bring correction to the body of Christ, who has been fed erroneous teachings about angels. Brenda functions as a teacher in the body of Christ and desires for God's people to enjoy the benefits that He has available to them by going into deeper depths of the things of God.

Not only has the Lord endowed her with immense revelation about the Kingdom of God pertaining to angels, the Lord is using Brenda as a fountain of revelation that will refresh the thirst God's people have for growing in greater understanding and revelation in the knowledge of Jesus Christ. At this juncture in God's *kairos* time, it is necessary for

God's people to understand what God is doing in the earth. I promise you that what God is doing does not exclude His *angels*. The book that you are about to read, *Awakening to Angels*, will increase your understanding of what God has bestowed upon us in the spirit realm.

I am certain you have heard of stories much like the scenario I used in the very beginning of this *Foreword*. You may relate to this scenario by person or third person experience or by having experienced a situation similar to the scenario. The thought, "There is no way", is a shared thought we all can recall ourselves thinking when we were in death-defying situations and we realized, "There was no way we should have survived! "The reason we survived is because God meant it when He promised in His word that, "No weapon that is formed against us will prosper" (Isaiah 54:17)!

There was no way we *should have* survived, but God made certain that no weapon formed against us succeeded in its mission (Isaiah 54:17). He released angels from heaven to protect and minister to us– not on our own accord, but because it was a part of His divine plan and His abundant love for us.

I pray that your understanding will be illuminated as you read and study this book. May you not only be illuminated, but may you be greatly informed of the highest protective service ever established in the heavens and on Earth. May you accomplish and complete supernatural assignments, not by your might and not by your power but by God's command of His angels, and by the Spirit of the Living God. I pray that you *Awaken to Angels*!

Donald Williams
Pastor, Miracle Center International Ministries, Maryland

Preface

As we enter into the final days upon the earth, we as a body of believers will begin to experience and hear eyewitness accounts of angelic encounters and visitations as never before. (Prophetic Word I received from God 2015)

Perilous times have begun. The church is under great attack by principalities, powers, rulers of darkness, and spiritual wickedness operating from high places (Ephesians 6:12). Satan has launched an all-out attack against the believers of Christ and has begun using his most powerful weapons.

Laws and statutes are being challenged daily that put believers at great risk for losing their religious freedoms. God did not leave us alone in the earth to fight these battles against spiritual wickedness but has assigned His angels charge over us to guard us in all of our ways (Psalm 91:11). We as believers must open our spiritual eyes to the supernatural power available to us from the Kingdom of God.

God desires to expand His Kingdom to the earth realm and that expansion requires our cooperation with His plan. God desires that His children on the earth have a thorough, biblical knowledge of His Kingdom, His angels and our role in expanding His Kingdom to the earth. Many believers are destroyed because they lack knowledge of the Kingdom of God and their inheritance of the right to experience heaven's wealth in the earth (Hosea 4:6).

Throughout the years, I've heard many incorrect teachings concerning angels. This has led believers to act in error when attempting to activate angels thereby limiting the work of angels on their behalf. When we as believers act erroneously regarding the things of the supernatural Kingdom of God, we limit the miraculous power of God in our lives.

Out of obedience to God, I am writing this book so believers will have access to a Bible-based teaching on God's angels and how to loose them from heaven to Earth to work on their behalf. As we begin to gain a biblical understanding of the Kingdom of God, His heavenly hosts and our need to welcome the supernatural Kingdom of God into the earth and into our lives, then we will begin to recognize God-ordained angelic encounters as never before.

My prayer is that as you read the chapters of this book and study the referenced Scriptures:

- Your faith in the supernatural Kingdom of God will increase.

- You will have knowledge of how to welcome the Kingdom of God into the earth realm.

- Your will develop a Bible-based understanding of God's angels.

- You will experience angelic encounters in your life as never before.

- You will begin to discern the presence of angels.

May the Kingdom of God invade your life and may you experience the supernatural Kingdom of God in the earth realm as never before.

Blessings,
Author Brenda K. Fields

Table of Contents

Introduction to Angels 1

    Introduction 3

    Why We Need Angels 5

    Types and Order of Angels 7

    Fallen Angels 12

    A Comparison of Angels and Spirit-Filled Believers 15

    The Nature of Angels 17

The Roles of Angels 27

    I ~ Angels – God's Messengers 29

    II ~ Guardian Angels 32

    III ~ Angels Go Before Us to Prosper our Way 36

    IV ~ Angels Deliver the Wrath of God 39

    V ~ Angels Bring Healing 42

    VI ~ Angels Warn Us of Danger 46

    VII ~ Angels Encourage and Strengthen Believers 49

    VIII ~ Angels Defend the Righteous 52

    IX ~ Angels Deliver the Righteous from Captivity 54

    X ~ Angels Provide for the Physical Needs of Man 56

XI ~ Angels Usher Believers into Their Final Resting Place 58

XII ~ Angels will Return with Jesus on the Day of Judgment 61

Angels and Authority in the Kingdom of God 63

I ~ Angels are Under God's Authority – Not Man's 65

II ~ The Believer's Authority over Fallen Angels 71

III ~ Angels are Not to Be Worshipped 73

IV ~ We are Not to Pray to Angels 76

V ~ Angels Must Be Discerned 78

Loosing God's Angels into Your Life 85

Loosing God's Angels into Your Life 87

I ~ Angels are Loosed through our Faith 89

II ~ Angels are Loosed through our Relationship with God 91

III ~ Angels are Loosed when we Confess the Word of God 93

IV ~ Angels are Loosed when we Pray 96

V ~ Angels are Loosed when We Cry Out to God 100

VI ~ Angels are Loosed when We Worship God 102

Conclusion 105

Angels are in Partnership with You to Fulfill Your Destiny 107

Introduction to Angels

Introduction

We all have our own ideas and beliefs concerning angels – some of us believe in them and some of us do not. The world has molded the image of angels to be cute little naked, chubby babies with wings who fly around doing good and spreading love everywhere they go. Although this sounds heavenly––it is not biblical.

The Bible references angels (angel, angels, cherubim, seraphim) over 380 times in the New and Old Testaments. None of these references describe a baby; rather, they describe mighty spirits sent to the earth by God to minister to those of us who will inherit salvation and to fulfill God-given assignments (Hebrews 1:14).

It is important that we as believers of God have a biblical understanding of the angels of God and do those things that will maximize their presence in our life. The Word of God is true and the Kingdom of God is in existence regardless of our beliefs.

As believers we were commanded to "seek first the Kingdom of God and his righteousness and all these things (our needs and desires) would be added unto us" (Matthew 6:33). Everything we need is found in abundance within the Kingdom of God. Not only our physical and material needs but also any supernatural assistance needed to accomplish our assignments here on Earth.

Angels are included in God's Kingdom. They are members of His heavenly host (residents of heaven) and under the authority of God and His son Jesus Christ. Angels have the ability to visit the earth realm on our behalf and exercise their supernatural abilities to accomplish those things that we in our human strength cannot do.

Angels are spirit beings (Psalm 104:4; Hebrews 1:7) created by God (Genesis 2:1) to execute His words (Psalm 103:20) and minister to those who will inherit salvation (Hebrews 1:14).

The Hebrew word *malak (H4397)* and the Greek word *aggelos (G32)* are both English translations of the word *angels*. Both Hebrew and Greek translations for *angel* means, "a messenger that is dispatched as a deputy specifically dispatched as a deputy by God" (Strong & Strong, 1984*)*.

As spirits, angels do not consist of flesh, blood and /or any physical substance. The Greek word *pneuma* is translated in English as "spirit" (In Thomas, R.L, 1981) and is defined as, "wind, breath or spirit. Angels are celestial (G4151) or *heavenly beings*" (Strong & Strong, 1984)

> *All flesh is not the same flesh: but there is one kind of flesh of men, another flesh of beasts, another of fishes, and another of birds. There are also celestial bodies and bodies terrestrial: but the glory of the celestial is one, and the glory of the terrestrial is another.* (1 Corinthians 15:39-40)

Angels are also referred to in scriptures as "sons of God" and "morning stars":

> *Now there was a day when the <u>sons of God</u> came to present themselves before the* LORD*, and Satan came also among them.* (Job 1:6)

> *Where wast thou when I laid the foundations of the earth? declare, if thou hast understanding. Who hath laid the measures thereof, if thou knowest? or who hath stretched the line upon it? Whereupon are the foundations thereof fastened? or who laid the corner stone thereof; When the <u>morning stars</u> sang together, and all the sons of God shouted for joy?* (Job 38:4-7)

Why We Need Angels

We are human beings made of flesh; yet "the battles that we fight in the earth realm are not against flesh and blood, but against principalities, against powers, against the rulers of the darkness of this world, against spiritual wickedness in high places" (Ephesians 6:12).

Satan and his dark angels are out to kill us and their goal is to separate us from the plan of God for our lives. Satan is a fallen angel–a spirit–and we cannot fight against a spirit in the flesh it must be fought spiritually. We are reminded in 2 Corinthians 10: 3-4, "For though we walk in the flesh, we do not war according to the flesh. For the weapons of our warfare are not carnal but mighty in God for pulling down strongholds...".

Our God is so faithful that He did not leave us here on Earth alone to fight against the enemy. He sent His Holy Spirit to dwell within and comfort us and He continually sends His holy angels to minister to and help us in our times of need (Hebrews 1:14).

When heavenly spirits visit the earth realm they are not subject to the laws of human nature but operate based upon the laws of God's Kingdom. Satan is always looking for an opportunity to destroy the believers even during times that we are not aware (1 Peter 5:8; Job 1:7). Because of the protection provided by the angels of God who are encamped all around we were guarded from the hand of the enemy (Psalm 91:11)

God has come that we "may have life and have it more abundantly" (John 10:10). God sends His angels to supernaturally assist those in the earth realm who will inherit salvation to aid us in fulfilling our purpose and walk in victory (Hebrews 1:14). It is important to know that angels are not sent out to help everyone on Earth, only those who will or have received the salvation of our God. So know that if God has sent an angel to assist you, then salvation is your inheritance. God's desire is to see us walk victoriously in all things and accomplish our purpose here on Earth.

The angels of God never lose a battle they are always victorious. They overthrew Satan and his angels in heaven and they continue to overpower them today. The angels of God supersede the angels of Satan 2:1 and they have the all-powerful, God-Almighty, our heavenly Father backing them. Satan does not have a winning chance against the angels of God.

Some of you may now wonder why you haven't had an angel ever assist you. I truly believe that angels have assisted all of God's sons and daughters here on Earth at one time or another. Angels are not always recognized by humans as an angel sent by God neither do they always appear as human (Hebrews 13:2). Just because you have never recognized the presence of an angel does not mean you have never benefited from their work.

As spirit-filled believers, we must resist Satan and be strong in our faith (1 Peter 5:8). We must allow the Kingdom of God to be established on the earth through us.

Types and Order of Angels

God is a God of order. When God established the New Testament Church; "He gave some to be Apostles, some Prophets, Pastors, Teachers and Evangelists; for the perfecting of the saints, for the work of the ministry, for the edifying of the body of Christ" (Ephesians 4:11). Just as God assigned various levels of authority and roles to believers within the church body, angels have diverse levels of authority and assignments within the Kingdom of God. However, all are working for the same purpose of assisting believers to accomplish their assignment of establishing the Kingdom of God in the earth (Hebrews 1:14).

The Bible does not tell us the exact order of the angels of God as it did for the church; although, by the scriptural description of various angels and the assignments they were sent to Earth to fulfill, we know that all angels are not ranked equally.

The angels that I will discuss in this section are those mentioned most frequently in the Bible: seraphim, cherub, archangels, princes, and the common ministering angels. There are some who would count members of the heavenly host as angels; however, the Bible did not call them angels but spirits so I will exclude them from this study.

Seraphim

The seraphim are an order of angels that have the responsibility of ministering continuously to God and are referred to as the "burning ones" or "ministers of flame": "Of the angels He says, 'He makes His angels spirits, and His ministers flames of fire,'" (Hebrews 1:7). (M.G. Easton M.A., D.D. (1897)

Isaiah described this order of angels as standing above the throne of God and continuously crying out to one another, "Holy, Holy, Holy" (Isaiah 6:3). In addition, he described their appearance:

> *In the year that king Uzziah died I saw also the Lord sitting upon a throne, high and lifted up, and his train filled the temple. Above it stood the seraphims: each one had six wings; with twain he covered his face, and with twain he covered his feet, and with twain he did fly.* (Isaiah 6:1-2)

Seraphim are mentioned only twice in the Bible and are one of two orders of angels described as having wings.

Cherubim

Cherubim are a group of angels who seem to be responsible for guarding sacred places. Cherubim (or cherub) are mentioned over 128 times in Scripture (cherubim 58 and cherub 70 times) and were assigned the responsibility of guarding the Garden of Eden, the Gate of the Lord's House and the Mercy Seat of the Ark:

> *So he drove out the man; and he placed at the east of the garden of Eden Cherubims, and a flaming sword which turned every way, to keep the way of the tree of life.* (Genesis 3:24)

> *And the Cherubims lifted up their wings, and mounted up from the earth in my sight: when they went out, the wheels also were beside them, and every one stood at the door of the east gate of the LORD'S house; and the glory of the God of Israel was over them above.* (Ezekiel 10:19)

> *And make one cherub on the one end, and the other cherub on the other end: even of the mercy seat shall ye make the cherubims on the two ends thereof. And the cherubims shall stretch forth their wings on high, covering the mercy seat with their wings, and their faces shall look one to another; toward the mercy seat shall the faces of the cherubims be. (Exodus 25:19-20)*

We learn in Ezekiel that Lucifer was a cherub prior to His fall: "Thou art the anointed cherub that covereth..." (28:14). Ezekiel and others vividly describe the cherubim:

- Cherubim are living creatures (Ezekiel 10:20).

- Cherubim have the likeness of man (Ezekiel 1:8).

- They usually appear in pairs (Exodus 37:8; Numbers 7:89; 1 Kings 6:23, 27).

- They have wings (Ezekiel 11:22, 25:20; Exodus 37:9; 1 Kings 8:7).

- Cherubs have two or more faces: ox, cherub, lion, eagle, and Man (Exodus 25:20; Ezekiel 1:10, 10:14, 41:18; 2 Chronicles 3:13).

- They have feet (Ezekiel 1:7).

- Wheels are associated with cherubim (Ezekiel 1:16, 10:9, 16, 19).

- They have the hands of man (Ezekiel 10:8).

- They can fly (Psalm 18:10; 2 Samuel 22:11).

- They stand on each side of the throne (1 Samuel 4:4).

- The Glory of the Lord arise from them (Ezekiel 9:3, 10:3-4, 10:19; Hebrews 9:5).

- They have the appearance of burning coals of fire (Ezekiel 1:13).

- They have the appearance of a flash of lightning (Ezekiel 1:13-14).

Ministering Angels

The most commonly discussed angels in the Bible are those sent to minister to and help those who will inherit salvation. These angels are very powerful and are our first line of defense against the forces of darkness. As noted in Daniel 10:13, although they are very powerful and are well able to assist us, when fighting against certain forces of evil they may at times require the assistance of the assigned archangel or chief prince for that particular region (Daniel 10:13).

Archangels and Princes

Archangels are believed to be angels of great authority; it is their voice in which the voice of the Lord is likened unto:

For the Lord himself shall descend from heaven with a shout, with the voice of the archangel, and with the trump of God, and the dead in Christ shall rise first. (1 Thessalonians 4:16)

There is only one angel in the Bible identified as an archangel; Michael. Because the angel Gabriel identified Michael as "*one* of the *chief princes*" we know that there is more than one chief prince (Daniel 10:13, *emphasis added*). Michael had the dual role of archangel and chief prince over the Hebrew people supporting the fact that archangels also serve the role of chief princes and are assigned to oversee specific regions and people (Daniel 10:21).

The chief prince (archangel) Michael was identified as a leader and strong force in various spiritual battles including the battle against Satan, who was also identified as the King of Tyrus (Ezekiel 28:12).

- Michael led the angels of God in the battle against Satan and His band of fallen angels (Revelation 12:7-9).

- Michael contended with Satan over the body of Moses (Jude 1:9).

- Michael was a strong force in assisting Gabriel in the Battle against the prince of the kingdom of Persia (Daniel 10:13).

In the fighting of spiritual battles, Michael had other angels under his command. He was the leader of battles and a strong force in contending with Satan and assisting other angels when spiritual forces of darkness were overpowering them.

Fallen Angels

And the angels which kept not their first estate, but left their own habitation, he hath reserved in everlasting chains under darkness unto the judgment of the great day. (Jude 1:6)

I will not devote much of this book to Lucifer and his dark angels; however, I do want you to understand that not all angels are good.

When we hear the word "angel", many of us think of those spiritual beings that are good and work for God to aid in our victory here on Earth; this is not totally so. There are those good, godly angels of God who are working on our behalf but there are also evil angels who have chosen to work for Satan to cause our demise.

All angels were originally created perfect; however they, like humans, have free will to choose whom they will serve. Not all of the angels continued serving their original positions as God's angels.

Lucifer was described as one of heaven's brightest stars. He served in the high position of a cherub that covered and sat on the highest mountain of God (Ezekiel 28:12-19). Lucifer had one of the highest angelic positions in heaven.

When Lucifer is depicted in the minds of many, they conceive an evil being with horns coming through his skull – this is not so. Lucifer was described as being "full of wisdom and perfect in beauty" (Ezekiel 28:12). Not only was Lucifer full of beauty but his covering consisted of every precious stone:

> *Thou hast been in Eden the garden of God; every precious stone was thy covering, the sardius, topaz, and the diamond, the beryl, the onyx, and the jasper, the sapphire, the emerald, and the carbuncle, and gold: the workmanship of thy tabrets and of thy*

pipes was prepared in thee in the day that thou wast created. (Ezekiel 28:13)

Lucifer became prideful in his own sight and deceived himself into thinking that he could actually rise greater than the Lord, God Almighty. We see this in Ezekiel, *"Thine heart was lifted up because of thy beauty, thou hast corrupted thy wisdom by reason of thy brightness"* (28:17).

Though Lucifer once occupied one of the highest places in heaven, God cast him out of heaven due to his pride. He fell onto the earth where he and the angels that chose to follow him now reside:

> *<u>I will cast thee to the ground;</u> I will lay thee before kings, that they may behold thee. Thou hast defiled thy sanctuaries by the multitude of thine iniquities, by the iniquity of thy traffick; therefore will I bring forth a fire from the midst of thee, it shall devour thee, and <u>I will bring thee to ashes upon the earth</u> in the sight of all them that behold thee. All they that know thee among the people shall be astonished at thee: thou shalt be a terror, and never shalt thou be any more.* (Ezekiel 28:17-19, emphasis added)

> *And there was war in heaven: Michael and his angels fought against the dragon; and the dragon fought and his angels, And prevailed not; neither was their place found any more in heaven. And the great dragon was cast out, that old serpent, called the Devil, and Satan, which deceiveth the whole world: he was cast out into the earth, and his angels were cast out with him.* (Revelation 12: 7-9)

Never again will Satan occupy heaven. He is forever doomed. One third of the angelic population chose to follow Lucifer by rebelling against God (Revelation 12:7-12). Satan and His angels, after being thrown out of heaven, are now on Earth doing the opposite of the angels of God. Satan and his fallen angels have purposed to spread the kingdom of darkness and therefore want to cause us to fail in establishing the Kingdom of God on Earth.

Although the enemy is out to destroy us, we as believers must know that our heavenly Father has given us the victory over Lucifer and his demonic followers.

> *He that committeth sin is of the devil; for the devil sinneth from the beginning. For this purpose the Son of God was manifested, that he might destroy the works of the devil.* (1 John 3:8)

> *And they overcame him by the blood of the Lamb, and by the word of their testimony; and they loved not their lives unto the death.* (Revelation 12:11)

A Comparison of Angels and Spirit-Filled Believers

Some people would have us believe that after death there is the possibility that men can be transformed into angels. Some have even proclaimed to have deceased loved ones watching over them. Others teach that aborted babies and deceased children become God's little angels; as consoling as this may sound, it is not biblical.

Angels and men are two distinct beings. Although we are both referred to as "sons of God" in our earthly state we are not equal to angels (Job 1:6, 2:1, 38:7; John 1:12; Galatians 4:6; Philippians 2:15; 1 John 3:1-2). Even after our resurrection from the dead we will not become angels but be "like angels" (Luke 20:35-36). There is a difference.

Angels were _created_ sons of God while we as born again believers will _become_ sons of the resurrection (Luke 20:36). As sons of the resurrection we will be equal in respect to authority and abilities to the angels of God.

The author of Hebrews notes a distinction between angels and the spirits of men made perfect (heirs of salvation):

> *But ye are come unto Mount Sion, and unto the city of the living God, the heavenly Jerusalem, and to an innumerable company of <u>angels,</u> To the general assembly and church of the firstborn, which are written in heaven, and to God the Judge of all, and to <u>the spirits of just men made perfect</u>...* (Hebrews 12:22-23)

As born again believers we inherit salvation, power, and authority in the earth realm from God. We cannot do the things that angels of God can do because they are more powerful and are not limited by the laws of physics (2 Peter 2:11). We have become the children of God but we are still made of flesh and blood (Romans 8:17). As flesh and blood, we have limitations; whereas, angels are not limited by the physics of Earth. Angels are therefore sent by God to assist us in those things that we, because of our human limitations, cannot accomplish alone.

Similarities between Angels and Man

Angels	Man
Angels were created by God (Genesis 2:1, Colossians 1:16)	Man was created by God (Genesis 1:27)
Have a choice in whom they will serve (Jude 1:6)	Have a choice in whom they will serve (Joshua 24:15)
Commanded to worship God (Hebrews 1:6)	Commanded to worship God (Matthew 4:10)

Differences between Angels and Man

Angels	Man
Created by the spoken Word of God (Psalm 33:6)	Made by God from the dust of the ground (Genesis 2:7)
Spirit being (Psalm 104:4, Ephesians 3:10)	Flesh and Blood created in God's image (Genesis 1:26)
Created to Serve (Hebrews 1:14)	Created to dominate (Genesis 1:26)
Do not receive forgiveness after sin (Jude 1:6, 2 Peter 2:4, Matthew 25:41; Ezekiel 28:12-19)	Jesus died that man would receive forgiveness of his sins (1 John 1:9; Proverbs 28:13; Titus 2:14; Isaiah 1:18)
Currently has a place assigned to them in heaven (Genesis 28:12)	Live on Earth, God is preparing a Place for us in the heaven (John 14:3)
Cannot reproduce; Their number remains constant (Matthew 22:30)	Were commanded by God to be fruitful and multiply (Genesis 1:28)
Angels always see the face of God (Matthew 18:10)	No man has ever seen God's face (John 1:18)
Never die (Luke 20:36)	Will eventually die (Hebrews 9:27)

The Nature of Angels

When Were Angels Created?

Although we do not know the exact order of their creation, from God's response to Job we know that angels were present before the foundation of the earth was laid, "Where wast thou when I laid the foundations of the earth? declare, [sic] if thou hast understanding....When the morning stars sang together, and all the sons of God shouted for joy?" (Job 38:4, 7).

We also know that angels were created prior to the creation of Adam and Eve because Satan had already fallen and was present in the Garden of Eden where he tempted Eve (Genesis 3).

Do Angels Obey God?

Angels obey the word of the Lord:

> *Bless the LORD, ye his angels that excel in strength, that do his commandments, hearkening unto the voice of his word. Bless ye the LORD, all ye his hosts; ye ministers of his, that do his pleasure.* (Psalm 103:20-21)

Do Angels Reside in Heaven?

The angels of God have an assigned place in heaven.

> *Take heed that ye despise not one of these little ones; for I say unto you, that in heaven their angels do always behold the face of my Father which is in heaven.* (Matthew 18:10)

> *And God heard the voice of the lad; and the angel of God called to Hagar out of heaven, and said unto her, What aileth thee, Hagar? fear not; for God hath heard the voice of the lad where he is.* (Genesis 21:17)

> *After these things I saw another angel coming down from heaven, having great authority, and the earth was illumined with his glory.* (Revelation 18:1)

Can Angels be Cast Out of Heaven?

Satan and one third of the angelic population lost their place in heaven after their rebellion:

> *And there was war in heaven: Michael and his angels fought against the dragon; and the dragon fought and his angels, And prevailed not; neither was their place found any more in heaven, And the great dragon was cast out, that old serpent, called the Devil, and Satan, which deceiveth the whole world: he was cast out into the earth, and his angels were cast out with him* (Revelation 12: 7-9)

> *And the angels which kept not their first estate, but left their own habitation, he hath reserved in everlasting chains under darkness unto the judgment of the great day.* (Jude 1:6)

Do Angels Travel to Earth?

> *And he saith unto him, Verily, verily, I say unto you, Hereafter ye shall see heaven open, and the angels of God ascending and descending upon the Son of man."* (John 1:51)

> *And he dreamed, and behold a ladder set up on the earth, and the top of it reached to heaven: and behold the angels of God ascending and descending on it.* (Genesis 28:12)

Are Angels the Only Inhabitants of Heaven?

Angels are among those included in the heavenly host created by God in Genesis 2 however they are not the only inhabitants of heaven. The term "heavenly host" is inclusive of all those that inhabit the heavenly realm. Although the angels are the most common of the heavenly hosts discussed, they are not alone.

> *And suddenly there was with the angel a multitude of the heavenly host praising God.* (Luke 2:13)

> *Praise ye him, all his angels: praise ye him, all his hosts.* (Psalm 148:2)

> *Bless ye the LORD, all ye his hosts; ye ministers of his, that do his pleasure.* (Psalm 103:21)

> *By the word of the LORD were the heavens made; and all the host of them by the breath of his mouth.* (Psalm 33:6)

> *"I have made the earth, and created man upon it: I, even my hands, have stretched out the heavens, and all their host have I commanded.* (Isaiah 45:12)

What Gender are Angels?

Angels are spirits (Psalms 104:4) and in the spirit realm there is neither male nor female (Galatians 3:28). When angels appeared in flesh they always presented themselves as male. This is not by any means to imply that angels cannot present themselves in the flesh as females.

Do Angels Have their Own Language?

Angels have a unique language. Paul makes a distinction between the tongues of men and the tongues of angels:

> *Though I speak with the tongues of men and of angels, and have not charity, I am become as sounding brass, or a tinkling cymbal.* (1 Corinthians 13:1)

Although angels have their own unique language, they have the ability to speak in any of the tongues of man. We must remember that angels are Gods messengers and when delivering a message to man they will always speak in a language that the recipient understands.

Do Angels Have the Bodily Functions as Man?

When angels appear as man they are capable of performing the activities of man. The angels of the Lord who appeared unto Abraham ate food, drank, and had their feet washed by Abraham.

> *And Abraham hastened into the tent unto Sarah, and said, 'Make ready quickly three measures of fine meal, knead it, and make cakes upon the hearth'. And Abraham ran unto the herd, and fetcht a calf tender and good, and gave it unto a young man; and he hasted to dress it. And he took butter, and milk, and the calf which he had dressed, and set it before them; and he stood by them under the tree, and they did eat.* (Genesis 18:6-8)

When these very angels appeared unto Lot, the men of Sodom were physically attracted to them and attempted to attack them in a sexual manner but were struck blind by the angels. (Genesis 19:5-11)

> *And they called unto Lot, and said unto him, 'Where are the men which came in to thee this night? bring them out unto us, that we may know them.'"* (Genesis 19:5)

Do Angels Marry?

Angels neither marry nor are they given into marriage (Matthew 22:30; Mark 12:25). We must remember that angels (in their heavenly state) do not possess a body – they are spirits. God instituted marriage after the creation of man as a remedy for his loneliness. Eve then became "bone of Adam's bone and flesh of his flesh" (Genesis 2:23). Angels possess neither flesh nor bones. Marriage was established strictly to satisfy the fleshly needs of man.

Do Angels Reproduce?

There is no Scripture in the Bible that supports that the angelic population will increase. God created angels and they do not reproduce nor do humans become angels after death. The angelic population remains constant.

After Satan and one third of the angels lost their place in heaven – the angelic population decreased drastically yet there were no additional angels created by God to take their place. God commanded man to be fruitful and multiply (Genesis 1:28). However, there is not a Scripture where He makes this command to the angels.

What is the Lifespan of an Angel?

After our resurrection we shall be like the angels and not subject to death (Luke 20:36). As terrible as the fight Michael and his angels fought against Satan and His angels, there was no reported loss of life nor was there any written report of physical injuries.

Angels are spirits and do not possess flesh; they are not subject to physical injury or death. Spirits remain forever.

How Powerful are Angels?

Angels are mighty and excel in strength: *Bless the LORD, ye his angels, that excel in strength, that do his commandments, hearkening unto the voice of his word* (Psalm 103:20).

Angels have supernatural strengths and abilities which were demonstrated on various occasions when they were sent to the earth realm:

- One angel of the Lord rolled back the stone that covered Jesus' tomb (Matthew 28:2).

- One angel of God unlocked the prison doors that held Peter captive: (Acts 5:17-20).

- One angel was sent by God to destroy the entire city of Jerusalem (1 Chronicles 21:15).

- Two angels were sent by God to destroy the cities of Sodom and Gomorrah (Genesis 19:13; 24, 25).

- One angel of the LORD went out and struck down one hundred and eighty-five thousand in the camp of the Assyrians. (Isaiah 37:36; 2 Kings 19:35).

- Angels of God delivered the plagues in Egypt (Exodus 12:13-30; Psalm 78:49; Hebrews 11:28).

Can a Man Overpower an Angel of God?

Even when angels appear as man they still remain more powerful and mightier than man (2 Peter 2:11). Jacob's battle with an angel of the Lord is a great example of this. As Jacob demonstrated it is possible to wrestle with an angel of the Lord who appears as man, but man cannot overpower them when they use their full strength.

> *And Jacob was left alone; and there wrestled a man with him until the breaking of the day. And when he saw that he prevailed not against him, he touched the hollow of his thigh; and the hollow of Jacob's thigh was out of joint, as he wrestled with him. And he said, Let me go, for the day breaketh. And he said, I will not let thee go, except thou bless me.* (Genesis 32:24-26)

Some teach that Jacob somehow won this battle against the angel of the Lord as he was granted his request. Although the angel was recorded having not prevailed against Jacob, the angel was still more powerful.

We must remember that angels of the Lord are sent out to help those who will inherit salvation, not to destroy them. Although the angel was tired of wrestling against Jacob, note that it only took one touch of the angel's hand to dislocate Jacobs' thigh socket. If one touch caused his thigh to become dislocated, imagine the damage Jacobs' body would have endured had the angel not been gentle with him. This angel of the Lord was not sent on an assignment to destroy Jacob therefore he could not have taken his life.

> *"Whereas angels, which are greater in power and might, bring not railing accusation against them before the Lord."* (2 Peter 2:11)

Do Angels have Names?

According to the Bible, God calls by name everything that He created on high:

> *To whom then will ye liken me, or shall I be equal? saith the Holy One. Lift up your eyes on high, and behold who hath created these things, that bringeth out their host by number: he calleth them all by names by the greatness of his might, for that he is strong in power; not one faileth.* (Isaiah 40:25-26)

Are Angels All Knowing?

Angels are wiser than man yet not all knowing as God.

> *Unto whom it was revealed, that not unto themselves, but unto us they did minister the things, which are now reported unto you by them that have preached the gospel unto you with the Holy Ghost sent down from heaven; which things the angels desire to look into.* (1 Peter 1:12)

> *But of that day and hour knoweth no man, no, not the angels of heaven, but my Father only.* (Matthew 24:36)

> *To the intent that now unto the principalities and powers in heavenly places might be known by the church the manifold wisdom of God, According to the eternal purpose which he purposed in Christ Jesus our Lord:* (Ephesians 3:10-11)

Are Angels Omnipresent?

Angels are not everywhere at all times as God; nor is one particular angel in the same location at all times. Angels travel in time. They arrive on the scene so quickly that you may think they were there all the time. When angels appeared in Scripture, God always <u>sent</u> them to the place of their assignment.

Do Angels have Wings?

Only two groups of angels were documented in the Bible as having wings. They were the seraphim (Isaiah 6:1-2) and cherubim (Exodus 25:19-20). John describes seeing angels fly around heaven:

> *And I beheld, and heard an angel flying through the midst of heaven, saying with a loud voice, Woe, woe, woe, to the inhabiters of the earth by reason of the other voices of the*

trumpet of the three angels, which are yet to sound! (Revelation 8:13)

How do Angels Travel?

Angels that made visitations to the earth realm were not described as having wings yet they were capable of flying. Daniel described the angel Gabriel as a man who came in swift flight; yet, he never mentions him having wings:

> *Yea, whiles I was speaking in prayer, even the man Gabriel, whom I had seen in the vision at the beginning, being caused to fly swiftly, touched me about the time of the evening oblation.* (Daniel 9:21-22)

Jacob described seeing angels ascend and descend from heaven to Earth by way of a ladder:

> *And he dreamed, and behold a ladder set up on the earth, and the top of it reached to heaven: and behold the angels of God ascending and descending on it.* (Genesis 28:12)

How Many Angels are There?

Angels are innumerable:

> *But ye are come unto mount Sion, and unto the city of the living God, the heavenly Jerusalem, and to an innumerable company of angels.* (Hebrews 12:22)

> *A fiery stream issued and came forth from before him: thousand thousands ministered unto him, and ten thousand times ten thousand stood before him: the judgment was set, and the books were opened.* (Daniel 7:10)

The chariots of God are twenty thousand, even thousands of angels: the Lord is among them, as in Sinai, in the holy place. (Psalm 68:17)

And I beheld, and I heard the voice of many angels round about the throne and the beasts and the elders: and the number of them was ten thousand times ten thousand, and thousands of thousands. (Revelation 5:11)

The Roles of Angels

I
Angels – God's Messengers

The word *angel* is derived from the Greek word *aggelos* which is defined by The New Testament Greek Lexicon (1999) as "an angel, an envoy, one who is sent, an angel, and a messenger from God" (Thayer & Smith).

God desires to communicate with His children and throughout the Bible we see Him delivering those messages to those on Earth by various means. He uses dreams, visions, prophetic gifting, prophets, and let's not forget–his messenger angels. Throughout the Bible, we read of God sending His angels to deliver messages from heaven to people on the earth.

A Message to Zacharias

Zacharias and Elizabeth prayed to God for a son. While in the Temple praying to God, an angel was sent by God to deliver a message to Zacharias concerning his prayers being answered:

> *And the whole multitude of the people was praying outside at the hour of incense. Then an <u>angel of the Lord appeared to him</u>, standing on the right side of the altar of incense. And when Zacharias saw him, he was troubled, and fear fell upon him. But the angel said to him, "<u>Do not be afraid, Zacharias, for your prayer is heard; and your wife Elizabeth will bear you a son, and you shall call his name John</u>. And you will have joy and gladness, and many will rejoice at his birth. For he will be great in the sight of the Lord."* (Luke 1:10-15, NKJV, emphasis added)

A Message to the Virgin Mary

An angel was sent by God to the Virgin Mary to deliver the message that she had been chosen to bear the Savior of the world:

> *Now in the sixth month <u>the angel Gabriel was sent by God</u> to a city of Galilee named Nazareth, to a virgin betrothed to a man whose name was Joseph, of the house of David. The virgin's name was Mary. And having come in, the angel said to her, "Rejoice, highly favored one, the Lord is with you; blessed are you among women!" But when she saw him, she was troubled at his saying, and considered what manner of greeting this was. Then the angel said to her, "Do not be afraid, Mary, for you have found favor with God. And behold, you will conceive in your womb and bring forth a Son, and shall call His name Jesus. He will be great, and will be called the Son of the Highest; and the Lord God will give Him the throne of His father David. And He will reign over the house of Jacob forever, and of His kingdom there will be no end."* (Luke 1:26-33, NKJV)

A Message to the Shepherds

An angel of the Lord was sent by God to announce the birth of Christ to the shepherds:

> *Now there were in the same country shepherds living out in the fields, keeping watch over their flock by night. And behold, <u>an angel of the Lord stood before them, and the glory of the Lord shone around them,</u> and they were greatly afraid. Then the angel said to them, "Do not be afraid, for behold, I bring you good tidings of great joy which will be to all people. For there is born to you this day in the city of David a Savior, who is Christ the Lord. And this will be the sign to you: You will find a Babe wrapped in swaddling cloths, lying in a manger." (Luke 2:8-12, NKJV)*

A Message to John

An angel of the Lord was sent to John to signify the revelation of Jesus Christ:

> *The Revelation of Jesus Christ, which God gave Him to show His servants—things which must shortly take place. And <u>He sent and signified it by His angel to His servant John</u>.* (Revelation 1:1, NKJV)

A Message to the Women at the Tomb

An angel of the Lord appeared to women at the tomb of Jesus to inform them that He had risen:

> *And it came to pass, as they were much perplexed thereabout, behold, two men stood by them in shining garments: And as they were afraid, and bowed down their faces to the earth, they said unto them, Why seek ye the living among the dead? He is not here, but is risen: remember how he spake unto you when he was yet in Galilee, Saying, The Son of man must be delivered into the hands of sinful men, and be crucified, and the third day rise again.* (Luke 24:4-7)

II
Guardian Angels

God has assigned an angel in heaven to watch over, minister to, and guard us in all of our ways (Psalm 91:11). Our assigned angel stands before the All-Knowing God of the universe and awaits directives concerning the work he must perform on our behalf (Matthew 18:10).

Can you imagine the love that Father God has towards us? Are you aware that we are His children and His heart felt desire for us is to help us accomplish our purpose here on Earth? Did you know that He actually sends angels from heaven with supernatural abilities to assist us in our weaknesses, encourage us, and minister to us when needed? It is comforting to know that the angels of the Lord are actually encamped all around us and are standing by to assist in our success (Psalm 34:7).

Concerning those who have humbled themselves before God as a little child, Jesus warns, *"Take heed that ye despise not one of these little ones; for I say unto you, That in heaven **their** angels do always behold the face of my Father which is in heaven"* (Matthew 18:10).

Angels are Not Always By Our Side

I have heard many teach that as believers our guardian angel is always with us; this is not supported in the Bible. Psalm 34:7 says that the angels of the Lord encamp around those that fear the Lord not that they dwell with them. To encamp signifies a temporary stay, not a dwelling place (Merriam-Webster, 2016).

In both the Old and New Testament, angels were always "sent" by God to fulfill their assignment. Angels always traveled to their destination, fulfilled their assignment and left the scene when their assignment was complete.

An Angel Freed Peter from Prison

King Herod had Peter thrown into prison and the saints prayed for him both day and night without ceasing (Acts 12). God answered their prayers by sending an angel to personally escort Peter out of prison. After being freed by the angel, Peter goes to the house where prayers were being sent up to God on his behalf. The young girl who answers the door excitedly announces to the others that Peter is at the door. The group finds this hard to believe and stated, "It is **his** angel" (Acts 12:15, emphasis added).

This Scripture supports the fact that the saints in the early church believed that Peter had an angel personally assigned to him and that particular angel was believed to have had some resemblance to Peter for the proposed mistaken identity to occur.

An Angel was Assigned to the Hebrew People

The fact that we have angels assigned to us is supported also in Daniel 10 when the angel of the Lord prepares to leave Daniel. The angel informs Daniel, in relation to giving him the understanding of his vision, *"I will shew thee that which is noted in the Scripture of truth: and there is none that holdeth with me in these things, but Michael **your** prince"* (Daniel 10:21, emphasis added).

In Daniel 12:1, Michael was described as *"the great prince, which standeth for the children of thy people,"* which helps us to also understand that Prince Michael was not in charge of Daniel alone but the "children" of thy people.

Michael was not the only angel in a *princely* position as when the angel visited Daniel he tells him of his delay being due to his being withstood by the prince of Persia and that "Michael, **one of the chief princes,** came to help me" (Daniel 10:13, emphasis added).

There is an archangel assigned over you just as there was over Daniel. You are not the only person a particular angel is assigned to

(Daniel 12). Your angel is in the presence of God awaiting the Father to send him to your aid (Matthew 18:10).

Angels are Assigned to the Seven Churches of Asia

God has seven angels assigned to the seven churches in Asia of which he revealed to John in a vision:

> *The mystery of the seven stars which thou sawest in my right hand, and the seven golden candlesticks. The seven stars are the angels of the seven churches: and the seven candlesticks which thou sawest are the seven churches.* (Revelation 1:20)

These seven churches were identified as the churches of: Ephesus (Revelation 2:1), Smyrna (Revelation 2:8), Pergamos (Revelation 2:12), Thyatira (Revelation 2:18), Sardis (Revelation 3:1), Philadelphia (Revelation 3:7), and Laodicea (Revelation 3:14).

The angel in heaven assigned to watch over us always stands in the presence of the All-Knowing God of the Universe, who knows every situation that we will have to encounter. Angels travel faster than the speed of light and will be on the scene before we can let out a scream for help. As children of the Most High God we must not be afraid to cry out to God in our time of need. God wants to help us to be successful in all things and He has angels eagerly waiting to respond to our needs.

Guardian Angels are Still Guarding Today

I remember it as though it was yesterday. Late one night I was walking to the store when a person approached me out of nowhere and questioned me about the phone I was holding in my hand. Unbeknownst to me there was a gang initiation in process and I immediately became their target. The person pulled out a gun, pointed it towards me and pulled the trigger. I remember falling to the ground – he then stood over, pointed the gun towards me and began unloading the gun shooting me seven more times.

Things happened so quickly that I didn't have time to pray or call on Jesus for help; yet, I witnessed the most amazing thing. An angel of God immediately appeared and literally stood over me protecting me from further harm. During the remaining gunshots, the angel of God stood with his back towards me, kneeled in front of me, and blocked every bullet that came in my direction thereafter.

I was rushed to the hospital where the doctors immediately began surgery. While in the operating room I remember looking around the room and saw the exact angel who had just shielded me from the gunfire standing there in the operating room nodding his head to me. I don't remember if the angel was male or female; he didn't have wings, he was translucent.

After the incident, as I was lying on the ground, I remember feeling as though I would die right there on the street that night. I cried out for God's help and he saved my life. Although I suffered many bodily injuries from the gunshots, God allowed me to be here today to share my testimony so others can experience His great love.

I continue to be amazed as I think about that moment today. God loved me enough to send an angel from heaven to protect and spare my life. We serve an amazing God who has the ability to immediately dispense angels to our rescue, to spare our lives from death. What a mighty God we serve!

Testimony of Minister Marcus Stanley
Richmond Virginia

III
Angels Go Before Us to Prosper our Way

Angels can be sent by God to go before us in our endeavors to prepare and make our way prosperous. There are times when we are in pursuit of accomplishing goals or fulfilling tasks and are not aware of the environmental conditions ahead or the condition of a person's heart of whom we may have to face. Throughout the Scriptures, angels are notorious for being sent ahead of men by God to prepare and prosper their way.

God Sent an Angel Ahead of Abraham's Servant

A great example of angels going before man to make his pathway prosperous occurred when Abraham sent his servant out to Mesopotamia to find a wife for his son Isaac. As the servant was preparing to leave he begins to indecisively question Abraham while wondering of the possibility that the woman may not be willing to return with him. Abraham then informs his servant that God would send an angel before him to make his way prosperous.

> *The LORD God of heaven, which took me from my father's house, and from the land of my kindred, and which spake unto me, and that sware unto me, saying, Unto thy seed will I give this land; he shall send his angel before thee, and thou shalt take a wife unto my son from thence.* (Genesis 24:7)

When Abraham's servant arrived in Mesopotamia he finds the environment conducive for his success. As he is praying to God for Isaac's wife, Rebecca arrives in his presence and is willing and ready to return with him and become Isaac's wife. The servant did not have to waste time in his search for Isaac's wife as the angel of the Lord had gone ahead of him lessening the effort and making him successful in his endeavor.

God Sent an Angel Before Moses to Prosper His Way

When God sent Moses out to various lands He sent an angel out before him to make his way prosperous.

> *Behold, I send an Angel before thee, to keep thee in the way, and to bring thee into the place which I have prepared. Beware of him, and obey his voice, provoke him not; for he will not pardon your transgressions: for my name is in him. But if thou shalt indeed obey his voice, and do all that I speak; then I will be an enemy unto thine enemies, and an adversary unto thine adversaries. For mine Angel shall go before thee, and bring thee in unto the Amorites, and the Hittites, and the Perizzites, and the Canaanites, the Hivites, and the Jebusites: and I will cut them off.* (Exodus 23:20-23)

> *And the Lord said unto Moses, Whosoever hath sinned against me, him will I blot out of my book. Therefore now go, lead the people unto the place of which I have spoken unto thee: behold, mine Angel shall go before thee: nevertheless in the day when I visit I will visit their sin upon them.* (Exodus 32:33-34)

When we are entering into new territories and endeavors, we as the children of God through Jesus Christ, can request of God to send His angels ahead of us to make our way prosperous.

The angels have the ability to lead us down the right path, prepare hearts of people prior to our arrival, and help us to be in the right place at the right time just as he did for Abraham's servant and Moses.

As I was traveling home from a business trip my prayer to God was that He sends His angel ahead of me to prepare my way and God did just that:

- I was identified as a pre-screened passenger at the airport and did not have to go through the normal security clearance to get on my flight.

- I was given an upgraded seat on the plane, which was larger and had more space.

- The scheduled planes I was to board were delayed for departing and returning; yet, I did not miss any flights.

- On the flight home I had an entire row to myself.

- I lost my driver's license and had no idea of how I would be able to get a rental car at the airport without it. The angels of God had gone ahead of me making it possible that the rental car company had a copy of my license on file so that I was able to rent the car.

I am thankful to God for sending His angels ahead of me to prepare my way. I am becoming more cognizant of the need to ask God to send His angels ahead of me before traveling and entering into endeavors.

Angels can make our way safe when we travel. They can re-direct our path when we are headed in the direction of danger and safely guide us when we know not the way. With danger being on every hand, we need the assistance of angels to go before us in all things. So as you prepare to enter new endeavors remember to always ask the Father to send His angels out before you to make your way prosperous.

Father God,
As I enter into this day
Send your angels ahead of me
To prosper my way and make my pathway straight

IV
Angels Deliver the Wrath of God

Although angels dwell in heaven where everything is perfect and good, they are at times sent by God to deliver judgments of diseases, plagues and death upon those who walk in disobedience.

You may ask the question "How could something as awful as sickness and disease come from such a wonderful, loving God?" God is a God of love and He demonstrated His love when He allowed His only begotten son Jesus Christ to die on the cross so that we (sinners) would have a right to eternal life in Him.

As loving as God's heart is towards us, there are certain things that He does not tolerate of which sin and disobedience are amongst. In Scripture we are provided with many occasions whereby God sent angels to deliver wrath upon both His children and their enemies.

Balaam's Disobedience

When Balaam disobeyed the Word of the Lord, God sent an angel down from heaven with permission to kill him if necessary:

> *Then the Lord opened the eyes of Balaam, and he saw the angel of the Lord standing in the way, and his sword drawn in his hand: and he bowed down his head, and fell flat on his face. And the angel of the Lord said unto him, wherefore hast thou smitten thine ass these three times? Behold, I went out to withstand thee, because thy way is perverse before me: And the ass saw me, and turned from me these three times: <u>unless she had turned from me, surely now also I had slain thee, and saved her alive.</u>* (Numbers 22:31-33, emphasis added)

David's Punishment for Disobedience

We know David to be a "man after God's own heart". As great as God's love was towards David and in as much as He favored him, he still had to suffer the judgment when He chose to disobey God. In 2 Samuel 24, we are told of a judgment David and the children of Israel endured due to David's disobedience. God sent an angel down from heaven to bring a pestilence upon the children of Israel:

> *So the Lord sent a pestilence upon Israel from the morning even to the time appointed: and there died of the people from Dan even to Beersheba seventy thousand men. <u>And when the angel stretched out his hand upon Jerusalem to destroy it, the Lord repented him of the evil, and said to the angel that destroyed the people,</u> It is enough: stay now thine hand. And the angel of the Lord was by the threshing place of Araunah the Jebusite. And David spake unto the Lord when he saw the angel that smote the people, and said, Lo, I have sinned, and I have done wickedly: but these sheep, what have they done? let thine hand, I pray thee, be against me, and against my father's house.* (2 Samuel 24:15-17, emphasis added)

The fact that God loved David did not hinder Him from sending the angel to bring judgment in the form of pestilence upon the people for his disobedience.

As much as God loves us today we are not immune from the wrath of God's judgment coming upon us when we choose to walk in disobedience. Now, I am not saying that all sickness and disease are caused by man's sin or disobedience to God but God does send angels upon the earth with assignments to bring disease, plagues, and death upon those who walk in unrighteousness.

King Herod Killed by an Angel of God

When King Herod refused to give God the glory after the people of his kingdom referred to him as a god, an angel of the Lord was sent to destroy him:

> *And upon a set day Herod, arrayed in royal apparel, sat upon his throne, and made an oration unto them. And the people gave a shout, saying, It is the voice of a god, and not of a man. <u>And immediately the angel of the Lord smote him</u>, because he gave not God the glory: and he was eaten of worms, and gave up the ghost.* (Acts 12:21-23)

John's Vision of the Seven Last Plagues

In Revelation 15, John tells of his vision in which God shows him seven angels who will be released by God to deliver wrath in the form of the seven last plagues upon the earth:

> *And I saw another sign in heaven, great and marvellous, seven angels having the seven last plagues; for in them is filled up the wrath of God. And the seven angels came out of the temple, having the seven plagues, clothed in pure and white linen, and having their breasts girded with golden girdles. And one of the four beasts gave unto the seven angels seven golden vials full of the wrath of God, who liveth forever and ever. And the temple was filled with smoke from the glory of God, and from his power; and no man was able to enter into the temple, till the seven plagues of the seven angels were fulfilled.* (Revelation 15:1, 6-8)

As believers, our only hope to avoid the seven plaques that are to come upon the earth is to remain in God's perfect will and under the shadow of the Almighty (Psalm 91:1). Obedience to His voice and faithfulness to Him is our only escape. God loves us and does not will that any of us shall perish but that we all come to repentance (2 Peter 3:9).

V
Angels Bring Healing

Just as God sends His angels with plagues and diseases to destroy the unrighteous, He also sends His angels to the earth realm to deliver physical healing to His people.

The Pool in Bethesda

In John 5, we are told of a pool in Jerusalem called "Bethesda" of which an angel came from heaven during a certain season and troubled the waters. The people of that city were aware that whoever was the first to step into the pool after the waters were troubled by the angel of the Lord would receive healing of whatever ailment they suffered.

> *Now there is at Jerusalem by the sheep market a pool, which is called in the Hebrew tongue Bethesda, having five porches. In these lay a great multitude of impotent folk, of blind, halt, withered, waiting for the moving of the water. For an angel went down at a certain season into the pool, and troubled the water: whosoever then first after the troubling of the water stepped in was made whole of whatsoever disease he had.* (John 5:2-4)

The people had become accustomed to the angel of the Lord making a visit during a certain season at a certain place and knew that supernatural healing occurred after the angelic visitation

The Bible doesn't say whether the healing came because an angel had touched the pool or that God sent the angel to the pool for the sole purpose of someone getting healed. It only notes that healing occurred after the visitations.

Multitudes of people lay on the five porches surrounding the pool so that they could be the first to step in after the troubling by the angel. It is important that we understand that angels themselves are not the healers. God is our Healer yet He uses His angels at times to transfer healing to the earth realm. Angels are not the only vessels through which God brings healing; He also uses Spirit-filled believers to be vessels through which His healing power flows.

Jesus Heals the Lame Man

Jesus demonstrated this when He takes notice of a lame man who sat at the pool of Bethesda but had no one to assist him in being the first to get in. Jesus immediately healed the man of his infirmity:

> *And a certain man was there, which had an infirmity thirty and eight years. When Jesus saw him lie, and knew that he had been now a long time in that case, he saith unto him, Wilt thou be made whole? The impotent man answered him, Sir, I have no man, when the water is troubled, to put me into the pool: but while I am coming, another steppeth down before me. Jesus saith unto him, Rise, take up thy bed, and walk. And immediately the man was made whole, and took up his bed, and walked: and on the same day was the Sabbath.* (John 5:5-9)

Angels of God Still Lead Us to Healing Today

Angels of God continue to make visitations to the earth realm for the purpose of delivering healing to God's people. This healing may occur through atmospheres or by personal encounters with an angel sent for the sole purpose of healing a specific individual.

Mr. John Barfield, a native of Tuscaloosa, Alabama, who now lives in Ypsilanti, Michigan, shared his personal testimony of how a visitation from God's angels led to his healing as a child:

In the black community of Kaulton Quarters in West Tuscaloosa, his family crowded his bedside in their shotgun house on the hill, armed with tearful prayers and home remedies.

"My father said, 'Johnny, no matter what we did. Your fever got worse,'" Barfield said.

On this particular day, in an almost unheard of occurrence, two white women walked down the streets of the black section of Kaulton Quarters, up the steps to the Barfields' home, and came to the 5-year-old's bedside.

"They said to my mother and father, 'We would like to help you.'" Barfield said.

One of the women wrote a note and an address and gave it to Barfield's father. The women instructed him to go as fast as he could to the address and give the note to the man who resided there. The women left with as much mystery as they arrived.

"My father did not have a car, so he ran all the way to the white section of Tuscaloosa and he gave the letter to the man," Barfield said.

The man, a doctor, came to the Barfield home and to the boy's bedside. He asked for strong black coffee for an all-night vigil. Barfield's fever broke in the morning. In a few days, Barfield was once again in the backyard playing with the other children as if he had never been sick.

Too sick to remember the strangers who came to his aid, Barfield asked his parents about the women. His Father's response was 'Johnny I don't know, 'Nobody in Kaulton Quarters had ever seen them before and no one had ever seen them since. We just came to the conclusion they were angels God had sent to spare your life."

He always ended that story saying, 'Johnny, there must be work that God has for you to do.'"

Mr. John W. Barfield, founder of The Bartech Group Inc.; Author of *Starting from Scratch: The Humble Beginnings of a Two-Billion Dollar Enterprise*; Ypsilanti, Michigan

VI
Angels Warn Us of Danger

Angels are sent to keep us from danger and can save our lives. God is all knowing and His desire is that we have an abundant life. We live in a time today when the enemy is throwing every dart he can to destroy the children of God. God wants to spare our lives. He wants us to live even when we are surrounded by enemies on every side.

With our governmental authorities passing laws that oppose the Word of God and threaten the rights of Christians there is sure to be destruction upon our nations. There are earthquakes to come in various places, plagues, wars and rumors of wars (Matthew 24:6-7). Even with all of the prophesied destruction to come, God is still well able to keep those who trust in Him.

Lot and His Family Warned of God's Plan to Destroy Sodom and Gomorrah

When God determined to destroy the city of Sodom; he sent his angels to warn Lot of the impeding destruction and to personally escort him and his family to safety:

> *And there came two angels to Sodom at even; and Lot sat in the gate of Sodom: and Lot seeing them rose up to meet them; and he bowed himself with his face toward the ground; ... And when the morning arose, then the angels hastened Lot, saying, Arise, take thy wife, and thy two daughters, which are here; lest thou be consumed in the iniquity of the city. And while he lingered, the men laid hold upon his hand, and upon the hand of his wife, and upon the hand of his two daughters; the Lord being merciful unto him: and they brought him forth, and set him without the city.* (Genesis 19:1, 15-16)

As God sent angels to lead Lot and his family out of a city that was about to be destroyed, He can do the same thing for us today. As it was for Lot and his family, it is up to us to obey the angels sent by God. If we lose focus of the protective power of God by focusing only on the danger around us then we too risk being destroyed.

Balaam Warned by an Angel before Making a Wrong Decision

Angels can be sent by God to warn us before making wrong decisions in our lives. When Balaam decided to disobey God, God's anger was kindled against him and God sent an angel of the Lord to keep him from doing the evil.

> *Then the Lord opened the eyes of Balaam, and he saw the angel of the Lord standing in the way, and his sword drawn in his hand: and he bowed down his head, and fell flat on his face.*
> *And the angel of the Lord said unto him, Wherefore hast thou smitten thine ass these three times? behold, I went out to withstand thee, because thy way is perverse before me: And the ass saw me, and turned from me these three times: unless she had turned from me, surely now also I had slain thee, and saved her alive. And Balaam said unto the angel of the Lord, I have sinned; for I knew not that thou stoodest in the way against me: now therefore, if it displease thee, I will get me back again.*
> *And the angel of the Lord said unto Balaam, Go with the men: but only the word that I shall speak unto thee, that thou shalt speak. So Balaam went with the princes of Balak.* (Numbers 22:31-35)

Joseph Warned by an Angel

God can send angels to warn us when our life is in danger. We don't know all things – but God does. We don't know the true intentions of a person's heart; yet, God knows the inward motives before they are manifest to us in the natural. When King Herod sought to destroy baby

Jesus, God sent an angel to Joseph in a dream to warn him to flee to Egypt:

> *And when they were departed, behold, the angel of the Lord appeareth to Joseph in a dream, saying, Arise, and take the young child and his mother, and flee into Egypt, and be thou there until I bring thee word: for Herod will seek the young child to destroy him.* (Matthew 2:13)

Our heavenly Father is well able to protect us in every situation we face. Our God is well able to keep those who are His whether we are in the middle of destruction sent by God over a sinful nation, about to carry out a wrong decision in our own life, or when others have plotted plans for our demise. As we walk in these final days upon Earth with destruction all around, know that God is all powerful and all knowing and He will keep us in perfect peace if our mind is stayed on Him. (Isaiah 26:3)

VII
Angels Encourage and Strengthen Believers

Have you ever been in need of encouragement or a good pep talk and all of a sudden out of nowhere someone comes by with the right words that give you the strength needed to go and face your next challenge? If so; then you may have been entertained by an angel.

Angels sent to Encourage Gideon

As God was preparing Gideon for battle, He sent an angel to his side to speak words to him that would build his confidence and help him to understand who he was in God.

Gideon was feeling as though God had abandoned him and the people of Israel when seemingly out of nowhere an angel of God appears and declares to him that "The Lord is with thee, thou mighty man of valor" (Judges 6:12).

Gideon began to question the angel as to how God could be with him in his current situation. He essentially asks, "Where are the miracles?" and the angel of God proceeds to inform Gideon that he would be used by God to deliver Israel from the hands of the Midianites (Judges 6:13).

Although the angel of the Lord referred to Gideon as a "mighty man of God" (Judges 6:12), Gideon didn't see himself that way. He began to inform the angel of God that he is from a poor family and is the least of all in his father's house. Gideon didn't seem to think much of himself or his abilities. He was in need of encouragement. The angel of the Lord then informs Gideon that he (the angel) would be with him and that he (Gideon) would smite the Midianites as one man. As the Scriptures go on Gideon is victorious in battle and was used by God to deliver Israel from the hands of the Midianites (Judges 6).

Angels Were Sent to Strengthen Jesus Christ After Satan's Attack

At some time in our lives we have all been in need of strengthening, even Christ. After Satan's unsuccessful attempt to tempt Jesus Christ after he had fasted 40 days in the wilderness, God sent angels to minister to Him.

> *Then the devil leaveth him, and, behold, angels came and ministered unto him.* (Matthew 4:11)

God is aware of our every need and in those times when we are weak and in need of strength our Heavenly Father is well able to send a ministering spirit to us in form of man and sometimes in the form of angels (Hebrews 1:14).

Paul says concerning the believer; "We are hard pressed on every side, but not crushed, perplexed, but not in despair; persecuted, but not abandoned; struck down, but not destroyed" (2 Corinthians 4:8). We have an adversary, Satan, who is always on alert seeking whom he might destroy (1 Peter 5:8) and he does not discriminate against which believers he will attack. If he was bold enough to come after Jesus Christ then surely he will not hold back on us. Praise God for the victory that we have in Jesus Christ.

Angel Sent to Strengthen Jesus Christ Prior to His Crucifixion

As Christ was nearing the time that He would be taken away and crucified on the cross he earnestly prayed to His Father that if He be willing let the cup be taken away from Him at which time the Father sent an angel to strengthen Him:

> *And he was withdrawn from them about a stone's cast, and kneeled down, and prayed, Saying, Father, if thou be willing, remove this cup from me: nevertheless not my will, but thine, be done. And there appeared an angel unto him from heaven, strengthening him.* (Luke 22:41-44)

God has given each and every one of us an assignment here on Earth and just as Jesus faced opposition from the enemy in fulfilling His call, we too will be opposed by the enemy. We must be imitators of Christ when we are faced with opposition and trust in our heavenly Father to see us through no matter how challenging the task.

Daniel Strengthened by An Angel

When the angel of the Lord was sent to give Daniel revelation to his vision, He lost his bodily strength and an angel with the likeness of a man touched him and his strength was restored. (Daniel 10:12-19)

Our heavenly Father is all-powerful and promises never to put more upon us than we are able to bear. He promises that with each temptation He would make a way of escape (1 Corinthians 10:13). God will never leave us to face our challenges alone. He has already given His angels charge over us to keep us in all of our ways and to hold us up lest we dash our feet against a stone (Psalm 91:11-12). The angels have been sent by God to partner with us and help us in fulfilling our call.

VIII
Angels Defend the Righteous

Angels Defend Hezekiah Against the Assyrians

God sends angels to deliver destruction upon those who attempt to bring destruction upon His children. In 2 Kings 19 and Isaiah 37 we are told of Hezekiah being threatened by King Sennacherib of Assyria.

King Sennacherib sent words to Hezekiah boasting of the many armies and people he and his army had overthrown in battle. He went as far as to enlighten Hezekiah that the god of the other people whom he destroyed did not defend them and warned Hezekiah to "not be deceived by His God" (2 Kings 19:10).

After receiving the message of King Sennacherib's blasphemy against his god, Hezekiah went unto the house of the Lord and prayed unto God. God answered King Hezekiah's prayers by sending an angel to destroy the army of King Sennacherib:

> *And it came to pass that night that the angel of the Lord went out, and smote in the camp of the Assyrians an hundred fourscore and five thousand: and when they arose early in the morning, behold, they were all dead corpses.* (2 Kings 19:35)

Angels Defend Elisha Against His Enemies

When Elisha was threatened; God sent a host of angels to defend him:

> *And when the servant of the man of God was risen early, and gone forth, behold, an host compassed the city both with horses and chariots. And his servant said unto him, Alas, my master!*

how shall we do? And he answered, Fear not: for they that be with us are more than they that be with them. And Elisha prayed, and said, LORD, I pray thee, open his eyes, that he may see. And the LORD opened the eyes of the young man; and he saw: and, behold, the mountain was full of horses and chariots of fire round about Elisha. (2 Kings 6:15-17)

God is still able to send angels to fight our battles today. As we are living in the last days upon the earth believers will face many individuals who are enemies to Christ. There are Christians around the world whose lives are being taken away because of their decision to serve God. These are battles that we cannot win of our own strength; we must employ the power of the angels to help us. As King Hezekiah did when he was facing the challenge of King Sennacherib, we must turn to God in prayer.

We must know without a doubt that our God is God and that He protects those who love and serve Him. Just as God sent an angel to destroy the enemy of King Hezekiah, He will send an angel to destroy those who oppose His children today. Our God is all-powerful and He is real.

IX
Angels Deliver the Righteous from Captivity

It is never too late for angels to rescue the believer out of the hands of their enemy even when they fall into captivity.

An Angel Rescued Daniel from the Lion's Den

God sent an angel to deliver Daniel from the lion's den:

> *Then the king arose very early in the morning, and went in haste unto the den of lions. And when he came to the den, he cried with a lamentable voice unto Daniel: and the king spake and said to Daniel, O Daniel, servant of the living God, is thy God, whom thou servest continually, able to deliver thee from the lions? Then said Daniel unto the king, O king, live forever. My God hath sent his angel, and hath shut the lions' mouths, that they have not hurt me: forasmuch as before him innocency was found in me; and also before thee, O king, have I done no hurt.* (Daniel 6:19-22)

An Angel Rescued the Apostles from Prison

God sent an angel to deliver the apostles from prison:

> *Then the high priest rose up, and all they that were with him, (which is the sect of the Sadducees,) and were filled with indignation, And laid their hands on the apostles, and put them in the common prison. But the angel of the Lord by night opened the prison doors, and brought them forth, and said, Go, stand and speak in the temple to the people all the words of this life.* (Acts 5: 17-20)

An Angel Rescued Peter from Prison

God sent an angel to rescue Peter from prison:

> *Peter therefore was kept in prison: but prayer was made without ceasing of the church unto God for him. And when Herod would have brought him forth, the same night Peter was sleeping between two soldiers, bound with two chains: and the keepers before the door kept the prison. And, behold, the angel of the Lord came upon him, and a light shined in the prison: and he smote Peter on the side, and raised him up, saying, Arise up quickly. And his chains fell off from his hands. And the angel said unto him, Gird thyself, and bind on thy sandals. And so he did. And he saith unto him, Cast thy garment about thee, and follow me. And he went out, and followed him; and wist not that it was true which was done by the angel; but thought he saw a vision. When they were past the first and the second ward, they came unto the Iron gate that leadeth unto the city; which opened to them of his own accord: and they went out, and passed on through one street; and forthwith the angel departed from him. And when Peter was come to himself, he said, Now I know of a surety, that the Lord hath sent his angel, and hath delivered me out of the hand of Herod, and from all the expectation of the people of the Jews.* (Acts 12:5-11)

God is concerned with the safety and protection of His children and there are no limits to His power. When we are faced with opposition we should fall down before God in prayer and know without a doubt that He is well able to send a legion of angels at any time to rescue us from the enemy's hand.

X
Angels Provide for the Physical Needs of Man

There are no limits to the helping nature of God's angels when man falls in need. Although angels are spiritual beings, they are capable of delivering the tangible physical needs of man.

An Angel of God Provides for Hagar and Ishmael

After being sent away from the place they knew as home, Hagar and Ishmael were in the wilderness preparing to die of starvation and thirst when the Lord hears the voice of Ishmael and sends an angel to provide for his needs:

> *And God heard the voice of the lad. Then the angel of God called to Hagar out of heaven, and said to her, "What ails you, Hagar? Fear not, for God has heard the voice of the lad where he is. Arise, lift up the lad and hold him with your hand, for I will make him a great nation." Then God opened her eyes, and she saw a well of water. And she went and filled the skin with water, and gave the lad a drink.* (Genesis 21:17-19)

An Angel of God Provided Food for Elijah

When Elijah was preparing to take a journey that the angel of the Lord described as "too great for him" (1 Kings 19:7), He was provided with two meals from the angel of God prior to his journey. These meals provided him with enough energy to sustain him for 40 days and 40 nights:

> *And as he lay and slept under a juniper tree, behold, then an angel touched him, and said unto him, Arise and eat. And he*

looked, and, behold, there was a cake baken on the coals, and a cruse of water at his head. And he did eat and drink, and laid him down again. And the angel of the Lord came again the second time, and touched him, and said, Arise and eat; because the journey is too great for thee. And he arose, and did eat and drink, and went in the strength of that meat forty days and forty nights unto Horeb the mount of God. (1 Kings 19:5-8)

None of our earthly needs are too great for God to fulfill. As believers in Christ, we must not base the fulfillment of our needs on our finances or the economy. We must totally trust in God who has more than enough of everything we need.

When there is a famine in the land our God is well able to send His angels from heaven to provide for us from heaven's supply.

Though he had commanded the clouds from above, and opened the doors of heaven, And had rained down manna upon them to eat, and had given them of the corn of heaven. Man did eat angels' food: he sent them meat to the full. (Psalm 78:23-25)

XI
Angels Usher Believers into Their Final Resting Place

After our life on Earth has ended our spirit must spend eternity in either heaven or hell. As believers our ultimate desire should be to see the face of God and forever dwell in His presence. To forever dwell in His presence requires that we leave our mortal bodies behind. Paul says that to be absent from our body is to be present with the Lord (2 Corinthians 5:8). After the death of born-again believers, the angels of God will carry us to our resting place.

As a nurse, I have witnessed people prepare to leave this world to enter their eternal resting place. Some exited this world in fear and dread while others left in peace. Those who knew their God and the power of His resurrection knew that they were entering a better place.

Stephen had the Face of an Angel

As believers in Christ, the more we allow our natural man to die and allow Christ to live within us the more of His spirit we become. Prior to Stephen's martyr as he stood before those who took his life, he was said to have had a face that looked like an angel (Acts 6:15). As Stephen neared death he did not fear and God allowed him to see the glorious place awaiting him:

> *But he, being full of the Holy Ghost, looked up stedfastly into heaven, and saw the glory of God, and Jesus standing on the right hand of God, And said, Behold, I see the heavens opened, and the Son of man standing on the right hand of God.* (Acts 7:55-56)

Lazarus Carried into Abraham's Bosom

After the death of Lazarus, the angels of the Lord carried him into the bosom of Abraham:

> *And it came to pass, that the beggar died, and was carried by the angels into Abraham's bosom: the rich man also died, and was buried; And in hell he lift up his eyes, being in torments, and seeth Abraham afar off, and Lazarus in his bosom. And he cried and said, Father Abraham, have mercy on me, and send Lazarus that he may dip the tip of his finger in water, and cool my tongue; for I am tormented in this flame. But Abraham said, Son, remember that thou in thy lifetime receivedst thy good things, and likewise Lazarus evil things: but now he is comforted, and thou art tormented.* (Luke 16:22-25)

Michael Contends with Satan over the Body of Moses

After the death of Moses, the archangel Michael contended with Satan over rights to his body:

> *Yet Michael the archangel, when contending with the devil he disputed about the body of Moses, durst not bring against him a railing accusation, but said, The Lord rebuke thee.* (Jude 1:9)

Angels Usher Believers into their Resting Place Today

The angels of God are faithful to be with us even after death and will usher the believer into the presence of our Lord and Savior Jesus Christ:

A good friend of mine shared with me her experience as her granddaughter neared death:

> *A group of us were gathered together praying for my granddaughter who had received a poor prognosis after being diagnosed with cancer. I remember the women of God praying*

and crying out to God for my granddaughter's healing, for we knew that the prayers of the righteous availed much.

We all took turns praying and I remember as it became one of the women's time to pray she had very little to say. I knew that this woman was a strong believer and was gifted prophetically to hear from God. After the group had finished praying I approached her to gain insight into what God had shared with her concerning this matter. I remember her sadly looking at me as she shared that as she was praying she saw angels of God gathering around my granddaughter and that they were there to carry her home to be with the Lord.

My granddaughter died shortly thereafter. Although it was hurtful to lose her knowing that the angels of God had carried her to be with the Lord gave me a sense of peace.

XII
Angels will Return with Jesus on the Day of Judgment

The angels of God will return with Jesus Christ on the Day of Judgment and have a role in judging those on the earth:

> *For the Son of man shall come in the glory of his Father with his angels; and then he shall reward every man according to his works.* (Matthew 16:27)

> *Whosoever therefore shall be ashamed of me and of my words in this adulterous and sinful generation; of him also shall the Son of man be ashamed, when he cometh in the glory of his Father with the holy angels.* (Mark 8:38)

The angels of God will gather righteous from amongst the unrighteous:

> *And then shall they see the Son of man coming in the clouds with great power and glory. And then shall he send his angels, and shall gather together his elect from the four winds, from the uttermost part of the earth to the uttermost part of heaven.* (Mark 13:26-27)

> *The Son of man shall send forth his angels, and they shall gather out of his kingdom all things that offend, and them which do iniquity.* (Matthew 13:41)

Angels will continue to ascend and descend from heaven to Earth until the end of time. As long as the earth remains the angels will make visitations to the earth realm.

As the elect of God, born again believers will join the angels of God in judging both the world and fallen angels:

> *Do ye not know that the saints shall judge the world? and if the world shall be judged by you, are ye unworthy to judge the smallest matters? Know ye not that we shall judge angels? how much more things that pertain to this life?* (1 Corinthians 6:2-3)

After our resurrection, as the elect of Christ we will be made equal with the elect angels and join them in judging those of the world. The elect angels of God will not stand before us in judgment, had sin been found in them then they would have become fallen angels and no longer considered amongst the elect.

Angels and Authority in the Kingdom of God

I
Angels are Under God's Authority – Not Man's

As men and women of God we must understand our rightful position in God's Kingdom. God is a God of order and His order must be followed to get His results. Kingdom order requires that every soul be subject to higher powers (Romans 13:1). According to the Word of God all power in heaven and Earth was given unto Jesus Christ not unto man (Matthew 28:18, 1 Peter 3:22).

In our current state on Earth, as born-again believers filled with the Holy Spirit, we have not been given the authority over God's angels. Angels are clean spirits under the authority of God and are not included in the "spirits" that born-again believers have been given authority over.

Man was made lower than the angels (Psalm 8:5, Hebrews 2:7, 9) and are therefore not in a kingdom position to directly command God's angels. Angels of God are sent by God to assist us in accomplishing our kingdom assignments here on the earth.

There has been much error taught to the church in regards to born again believers having authority over angels. Many times I have heard Christians praying and attempting to directly command God's angels to do something – this is **not** biblical. Just as Jesus did not have the authority as man to directly command the angels of God neither do we.

Positions in the Kingdom of God must be respected. When we attempt to command those that are not beneath us in the kingdom we disrespect God's order of authority.

God never gave man the authority over the heavens or anything within it – including angels. As man, we remain a little lower than the angels and must do as Jesus Christ did prior to His resurrection and go through those with the authority over heavenly beings, God and His son Jesus Christ, to request angelic assistance.

Unlike man, angels always see the face of God (Matthew 18:10; 1 Timothy 3:16). John proclaims several times that no man has ever seen the face or form of God (John 1:18; John 5:37; 1 John 4:12). If man was created of a higher order than angels and had the authority to give them commands or assignments then why would God allow angels the ability to see Him and not man (1 Timothy 3:16)? Furthermore, if man is greater in authority than the angels of God then why do angels have the benefit of residing in the heavenly realm while we as born-again believers remain here on the earth?

When we look at the military order of authority never do we see lower officials making commands of the higher officials, they understand their position. I noticed in watching military personnel that when a person lacking authority over them gives them a command they do not move but remain in position to the point of ignoring the unauthorized commander.

This is the very position that angels take when we as man make direct commands of them: they don't move. They understand who their commander is and they respect His authority. Just as military personnel refuse to move until they get the command from their authorized commander, angels do not move until they get their command from God.

When Joshua the high priest was standing before the angel of the Lord and Satan began to oppose him over the body of Moses, it was the Lord whom the angel of God said to rebuke Satan:

> *And the Lord said unto Satan, The Lord rebuke thee, O Satan; even the Lord that hath chosen Jerusalem rebuke thee: is not this a brand plucked out of the fire?* (Zechariah 3:2)

When Satan attempts to devour that which belongs to the tither it is the Lord who will rebuke the devourer for our sakes:

> *And I will rebuke the devourer for your sakes, and he shall not destroy the fruits of your ground; neither shall your vine cast her fruit before the time in the field, saith the Lord of hosts.* (Malachi 3:11)

Jesus was the example that we as believers are to imitate in our lifestyle. As powerful as Jesus was when He walked the earth as man; never did he claim to have the authority over the angels of God. Prior to His resurrection from the dead, Jesus was a little lower than the angels, after the resurrection He was made "so much better than the angels" (Hebrews 1:1-4).

In no Scripture is this demonstrated greater than in Matthew 26:53 when Jesus is about to be taken away and crucified. As his disciples attempt to physically attack His accusers, He informs them that He could pray to His Father who would immediately send to Him more than twelve legions of angels.

> *Thinkest thou that I cannot now pray to my Father, and he shall presently give me more than twelve legions of angels?* (Matthew 26:53)

It is very important that we understand that as a man in the flesh, Jesus had to go through the Father in heaven to request angelic assistance and never does He claim the ability to directly command the angels of God. As the greatest man to walk the earth, Jesus was still a little lower than the angels (Hebrews 2:6-9; Psalm 8:5) and therefore did not have the authority to directly command angels.

Satan himself was aware of the need for Jesus to go through His Father for angelic assistance as voiced when he attempted to deceive Jesus:

> *Then the devil took Him up into the holy city, set Him on the pinnacle of the temple, and said to Him, "If You are the Son of God, throw Yourself down. For it is written: <u>'He shall give His angels charge over you,</u> 'and 'In their hands they shall bear you up, Lest you dash your foot against a stone.'" Jesus said to him,*

> *"It is written again, 'You shall not tempt the Lord your God.'"*
> (Matthew 4:5-7, NKJV, emphasis added)

After Jesus' death, burial and resurrection from the dead he received authority from the Father over the angels. Peter further explains that it was "through the resurrection of Jesus Christ, who has gone into heaven and is at the right hand of God, angels and authorities and powers having been made subject to Him" (1 Peter 3:21-22, NKJV).

It was through His resurrection from the dead that the angels of God were made subject to Jesus Christ. Angels are heavenly beings who are given assignments on the earth. They are therefore subject to Jesus Christ because He has been given the authority over things in both the heavens and on the earth.

> *God, who at various times and in various ways spoke in time past to the fathers by the prophets, has in these last days spoken to us by His Son, whom He has appointed heir of all things, through whom also He made the worlds; who being the brightness of His glory and the express image of His person, and upholding all things by the Word of His power, when He had by Himself purged our sins, sat down at the right hand of the Majesty on high, having become so much better than the angels, as He has by inheritance obtained a more excellent name than they.* (Hebrews 1:1-4, NKJV)

Our Savior, Jesus Christ, has authority over all things in heaven and in Earth. None of the angels were ever called God's "son" nor were any ever invited to sit at the right hand of God. All power is in His hand and all angels are now under His direct command.

> *For unto which of the angels said he at any time, Thou art my Son, this day have I begotten thee? And again, I will be to him a Father, and he shall be to me a Son? And again, when he bringeth in the first begotten into the world, he saith, And let all the angels of God worship him. And of the angels he saith, Who maketh his angels spirits, and his ministers a flame of fire. But unto the Son he saith, Thy throne, O God, is for ever and ever: a*

sceptre of righteousness is the sceptre of thy kingdom. (Hebrews 1:5-8)

"And Jesus came and spake unto them, saying, All power is given unto me in heaven and in Earth." (Matthew 28: 18)

Angels get their commands from God and His son Jesus Christ only. Born-again believers have not been given this authority. Believers can however do as Jesus Christ did prior the His resurrection and request angelic assistance from those in charge of the angels: God through His son Jesus Christ.

After Jesus' resurrection from the grave, He received a promotion in heaven. After our resurrection from death, we too will receive a heavenly promotion. We will not be equal to the level of Jesus Christ; however, we will be equal to the angels. (Luke 20:35-36)

It is important that Christians understand that this equality we will have with the angels of heaven does not occur until we are resurrected from the dead. Just as Jesus was positioned lower than the angels of God when He walked the Earth as man, so are we upon this Earth until our resurrection. (Hebrews 2:7, Psalms 8:5)

Angels are Sent to Help Us – Not Take Our Place

The angels of God are sent to assist us, not take our place and do the work that we have been assigned by God to complete here on the earth. Many times I have witnessed Spirit-filled believers ask God to send angels to do work that they themselves were assigned to complete.

I myself have been a violator as well. On one occasion a friend called and informed me that she was out on the interstate about 20 miles from my house with a flat tire and didn't have anyone to call for aid. I immediately called my roadside service to assist her but I would have to be on site to receive the service. Honestly, I didn't feel like driving 20 miles just to wait on roadside assistance so I began to pray that God would supernaturally send an angel to her aid to fix the flat tire.

After waiting for another phone call from her to say that someone had arrived to fix her tire, God quickly convicted me and reminded me that as a Spirit-filled believer, it was my responsibility to do all that I could to aid my sister in this situation. He would not send angels to do what I had the capability of doing with my own hands. I immediately got in my car and proceeded to the scene to aid my sister in Christ.

II
The Believer's Authority over Fallen Angels

When Satan and his fallen angels were cast out of heaven onto the earth, they lost their place of estate in heaven in addition to their place of authority in the heavenly realms (Jude 1:6). Jesus Christ, after His resurrection from the grave, was given all power and authority in the heavens and the earth. Satan and his fallen angels are now under Christ's authority because Christ holds all power and authority (Matthew 28:18).

As Holy Spirit filled believers, Jesus Christ has given us the authority over unclean spirits (demons, fallen angels). Satan and his fallen angels are now subject to us just as they are to Jesus Christ, and they have to obey our commands:

> *And when he had called unto him his twelve disciples, <u>he gave them power against unclean spirits, to cast them out,</u> and to heal all manner of sickness and all manner of disease.* (Matthew 10:1, emphasis added)

> *And the seventy returned again with joy, saying, Lord, <u>even the devils are subject unto us through thy name</u>. And he said unto them, I beheld Satan as lightning fall from heaven. Behold, <u>I give unto you power to tread on serpents and scorpions, and over all the power of the enemy: and nothing shall by any means hurt you.</u> Notwithstanding in this rejoice not, that the spirits are subject unto you; but rather rejoice, because your names are written in heaven.* (Luke 10:17-20, emphasis added)

To walk in our God given authority over unclean spirits, we must be subject to Jesus Christ as our higher authority and recognize our authority through Jesus Christ. Understand this: **The more we submit ourselves under the authority of Jesus Christ, the greater spiritual authority we will walk in as a believer.**

When the disciples attempted to cast a demon out of a young boy, the demon would not obey the disciples and flee. When Jesus arrived on the scene, the boy's father tells Jesus that the disciples were unable to cast out the demon. Jesus commands the demon to come out of the boy and it immediately obeys and leaves him. When the disciples inquired of Jesus as to why they could not cast it out, Jesus informs them that "this kind cometh out only by fasting and praying" (Matthew 17:14-22).

Prayer and fasting sensitizes us to the spirit of God and gives us greater awareness of our authority in the spirit realm. The more of Christ we allow to dwell within us the more authority we can exercise as a believer over the enemy and his band of fallen angels.

The sons of Sceva (Acts 19:11-20) attempted to cast out demonic spirits as they had observed Paul but were overpowered by the demons. Although the sons of Sceva imitated Paul by using the name of Jesus to command the evil spirits to come out, Christ Jesus had not granted them this authority and the demonic spirits were aware of this.

The level of our authority in the Kingdom of God is directly dependent upon our relationship with the Father. The greater our relationship with God through Christ Jesus the more power and authority we can operate in. The more of our life we surrender to God the more room we give the Holy Spirit to abide and flourish within us. Those who know their God shall do exploits in establishing the Kingdom of God here on the earth (Daniel 11:32).

The sons of Sceva did not know Christ personally, they were imitating what they saw Paul doing and they found out very quickly that it took more than imitating Paul's actions to cast out evil spirits.

Paul's authority over evil spirits was not just based upon his using the name of Jesus alone but upon his relationship with Christ and living a life totally surrendered to God. Demonic spirits recognize those whose spirits are surrendered to God and who walk in faith. We must daily build ourselves up in our holiest faith and pray in the Holy Spirit (Jude 20).

III
Angels are Not to Be Worshipped

As amazing as it is to be entertained by an angel from heaven–especially in their heavenly state – they are not to be worshipped.

As human beings we can become so amazed at the presence of an angel that we may fall down on our knees in awe. We must remember that all honor, glory, and worship belong to God alone. The angels of God are aware of this. They know that they were created by God and for God's use. They understand whose they are and that all that they are in their best state is nothing compared with the splendor of God. This is why the angels cry "holy, holy, holy is the Lord of hosts: the whole Earth is full of his glory," (Isaiah 6:3) when speaking of God.

Lucifer could not behold his own beauty and splendor as an angel of God but became lifted up in pride and was thrown out of heaven. As an angel of God, Satan was described in Ezekiel 28:12-13:

> *Thus saith the Lord God; Thou sealest up the sum, full of wisdom, and perfect in beauty. Thou hast been in Eden the garden of God; every precious stone was thy covering, the sardius, topaz, and the diamond, the beryl, the onyx, and the jasper, the sapphire, the emerald, and the carbuncle, and gold: the workmanship of thy tabrets and of thy pipes was prepared in thee in the day that thou wast created.* (Ezekiel 28:12-13)

As we discussed earlier, Satan's biggest problem was that he allowed pride to rule and thought himself equal to God and deserving of worship. Not only did he deceive himself, but one-third of the angels of heaven followed after him. God will not share his glory with anyone neither does He tolerate pride. We must be sure to not allow pride to get in front of our relationship with God.

The angels of God recognize and respect God's authority and His omnipotent power. They understand that God created them and that all worship belongs to Him.

John's Correction

When John began to fall down and worship an angel during an angelic encounter the angel of the Lord quickly corrected him:

> *And I John saw these things, and heard them. And when I had heard and seen, I fell down to worship before the feet of the angel which shewed me these things. Then saith he unto me, See thou do it not: for I am thy fellow servant, and of thy brethren the prophets, and of them which keep the sayings of this book: worship God.* (Revelation 22:8-9)

Monoah Warned Against Worshiping an Angel

When Samson's parents were visited by an angel, His father told the angel that he would offer up a sacrifice to which the angel of the Lord replied:

> *"Though thou detain me, I will not eat of thy bread: and if thou wilt offer a burnt offering, thou must offer it unto the Lord". For Manoah knew not that he was an angel of the Lord.* (Judges 13:16)

As believers in Christ we are commanded to worship God and God alone. The Church of Colossians seemed to have become involved in the worship of angels to which Paul warned:

> *Let no man beguile you of your reward in a voluntary humility and worshiping of angels, intruding into those things which he hath not seen, vainly puffed up by his fleshly mind.* (Colossians 2:18)

The error made by man is the tendency to worship the created rather than the Creator. We see the greatness of angels compared to us and lose sight of God. Angels of God are aware of man's weakness in this area. I believe that this is the very reason that angels of God avoid giving their names to those whom they visit. The angel who visited Manaoh and Jacob demonstrates this. When Manaoh asked the angel of the Lord his name so that he and his wife might honour him (Judges 13:17), the angel of the Lord responded, *"Why askest thou thus after my name, seeing it is secret?"* (Judges 13:18) When Jacob asked an angel his name, the angel responded similarly, *"Wherefore is it that thou dost ask after my name?"* (Genesis 32:29)

As glorious as the angels appear they are nothing in comparison to the beauty of our Savior Jesus Christ. Considering our amazement with the appearance of the angels of God in their splendor, can you imagine the glory we will behold when we look upon the face of our Lord and Savior Jesus Christ? On that glorious day we will only be able to proclaim and declare as the angels **"Holy, Holy, Holy!"** (Isaiah 6:3)

IV
We are Not to Pray to Angels

As I was reviewing books at a bookstore, I noticed a book that included the names of different angels, their assigned responsibilities, and how we can pray to each of these angels for particular needs. Not only is this unbiblical but it shows a level of ignorance to the work of God and a lack of knowledge of the Power provided to us through Christ's death, burial, and resurrection.

Through Christ's death, burial, and resurrection we were granted direct access to the Father. Why would a Spirit-filled believer go to a created being to request something when they have access to the very source that created all beings and supplies all needs?

> *For through him we both have access by one Spirit unto the Father.* (Ephesians 2:18)

> *Therefore being justified by faith, we have peace with God through our Lord Jesus Christ: By whom also we have access by faith into this grace wherein we stand, and rejoice in hope of the glory of God.* (Romans 5:1-2)

Angels are created beings. They do not have the authority to grant unto us anything without God's permission. Everything in God's Word is already promised to us for the asking. During this study of Scripture related to angels, in no place in the Bible did I find where God instructed man to pray to angels for the desires of their heart; we were always directed to pray to our heavenly Father:

> *After this manner therefore pray ye: Our Father which art in heaven, Hallowed be thy name.* (Matthew 6:9)

> *Let us therefore **come boldly** unto the throne of grace that we may obtain mercy, and find grace to help in time of need.* (Hebrew 4:16)

> *In my distress I called upon the LORD, and cried unto my God: he heard my voice out of his temple, and my cry came before him, even into his ears.* (Psalm 18:6)

Of the innumerable company of angels in existence isn't it amazing that God only saw fit that we knew the names of four: Gabriel (Daniel 8:16), Michael (Daniel 10:5-20, 12:1; Jude 9; Rev. 12:7), Lucifer (Isaiah 14:12-15), and Abaddon (Rev. 9:11)? If God desired that we go to the angels in prayer then why did He not include their names and individual responsibilities in Scripture? Why would a loving Father leave the believer void of such valuable information? Because praying to an angel is not the will of Father God for the believer.

Prayer is a form of worship. It exalts the one we are praying to. Just as the angels of God reject our worship, they reject any prayers directed up to them. We are commanded to worship the Lord our God and serve Him only (Matthew 4:10; Luke 4:8).

V
Angels Must Be Discerned

As believers, we must pray that God will open our spiritual eyes and ears that we see and hear the voices of angels and not miss angelic visitations in our life. Angels always come with purpose and to fully appreciate them there must be recognition of their presence.

We must not assume that all angels or spirits are from God but discern whether the spirit be from God or Satan (Hebrews 5:14). Satan, a fallen angel, transforms himself as an angel of light (2 Corinthians 11:14) and unless we exercise our spiritual discernment we can be deceived.

If an angel is from God their message and actions will always align with the Word of God. Angels, like man, have a choice in whom they will serve and not all of them choose to serve God (Jude 6). Paul warns us that if he or any angel from heaven teaches anything that opposes the Word of God they are accursed (Galatians 1:8). John warns us to not believe every spirit but informs us to try the spirits to examine whether they are of God:

> *Beloved, believe not every spirit, but try the spirits whether they are of God: because many false prophets are gone out into the world. Hereby know ye the Spirit of God: Every spirit that confesseth that Jesus Christ is come in the flesh is of God: And every spirit that confesseth not that Jesus Christ is come in the flesh is not of God: and this is that spirit of antichrist, whereof ye have heard that it should come; and even now already is it in the world. Ye are of God, little children, and have overcome them: because greater is he that is in you, than he that is in the world.* (1 John 4:1-4)

When angels appeared on Earth, man did not always discern that they were angels of God. As believers we must ask God to open our spiritual eyes that we will not miss the awareness of angelic encounters (Hebrews 13:2).

Just because you are not aware of a personal encounter with an angel does not hinder the angel from working on your behalf. They will fulfill their assignment. Our awareness of these encounters will, however, increase our faith and give us confidence that we are making right decisions in response to their directives or purpose.

Angels may not appear before you dressed in white apparel and flying around in the air. Most of the angels who visit Earth for the purpose of helping people usually appeared clothed in human flesh. As believers we also must open our spirit to receive angels of God through whatever means they appear. They may speak from the heavens or speak through a telephone call or an email. They may come to your front door or sit beside you on a plane. However they appear they always come to help us.

As Man

The angels that appeared to Abraham (Genesis 18) and Lot (Genesis 19) were in the form of men. Yet, there was something about them that made Abraham and Lot know that they were angels of the Lord because both men bowed down before them and referred to them as "Lord":

> *Then the Lord appeared to him by the terebinth trees of Mamre, as he was sitting in the tent door in the heat of the day. So he lifted his eyes and looked, and behold, three men were standing by him; and when he saw them, he ran from the tent door to meet them, and bowed himself to the ground, and said, "My Lord, if I have now found favor in Your sight, do not pass on by Your servant.* (Genesis 18:1-3, NKJV)

> *Now the two angels came to Sodom in the evening, and Lot was sitting in the gate of Sodom. When Lot saw them, he rose to meet them, and he bowed himself with his face toward the ground. And he said, "Here now, my Lords, please turn in to your*

servant's house and spend the night, and wash your feet; then you may rise early and go on your way." (Genesis 19:1-2, NKJV)

Out of this World Appearance

In contrast, the angel that appeared to Daniel was described in a manner that one could not mistake the fact that he was not of this world:

Then I lifted up mine eyes, and looked, and behold a certain man clothed in linen, whose loins were girded with fine gold of Uphaz: His body also was like the beryl, and his face as the appearance of lightning, and his eyes as lamps of fire, and his arms and his feet like in colour to polished brass, and the voice of his words like the voice of a multitude. (Daniel 10:5-6)

As a Voice from Heaven

In different occasions in Scripture those on Earth heard their message spoken directly from heaven. As Abraham was in the process of offering up his son Isaac as a sacrifice to God the angel of the Lord spoke to him from heaven:

And Abraham stretched forth his hand, and took the knife to slay his son. And the angel of the Lord called unto him out of heaven, and said, Abraham, Abraham: and he said, Here am I. And he said, Lay not thine hand upon the lad, neither do thou anything unto him: for now I know that thou fearest God, seeing thou hast not withheld thy son, thine only son from me. (Genesis 22:10-12)

An angel of God spoke blessings from God upon Abraham from the heavens:

Then the Angel of the Lord called to Abraham a second time out of heaven, and said: "By Myself I have sworn, says the Lord,

> *because you have done this thing, and have not withheld your son, your only son— blessing I will bless you, and multiplying I will multiply your descendants as the stars of the heaven and as the sand which is on the seashore; and your descendants shall possess the gate of their enemies. In your seed all the nations of the earth shall be blessed, because you have obeyed My voice."* (Genesis 22:15-18, NKJV)

After Abraham sent Hagar and his son, Ishmael, away, an angel of God spoke a message to her directly from heaven concerning God's provision for her and her son.

> *And God heard the voice of the lad; and the angel of God called to Hagar out of heaven, and said unto her, What aileth thee, Hagar? fear not; for God hath heard the voice of the lad where he is.* (Genesis 21:17)

In Dreams and Visions

Angels can appear to us in our dreams while we are in deep sleep and our spirits are open. The angel of the Lord appeared to Joseph in a dream on several occasions concerning the birth of Christ and his ongoing safety:

> *But while he thought on these things, behold, the angel of the Lord appeared unto him in a dream, saying, Joseph, thou son of David, fear not to take unto thee Mary thy wife: for that which is conceived in her is of the Holy Ghost.* (Matthew 1:20)

> *And when they were departed, behold, the angel of the Lord appeareth to Joseph in a dream, saying, Arise, and take the young child and his mother, and flee into Egypt, and be thou there until I bring thee word: for Herod will seek the young child to destroy him.* (Matthew 2:13)

The angel of the Lord appeared to Cornelius in a vision with a message concerning sending men to Peter:

He saw in a vision evidently about the ninth hour of the day an angel of God coming in to him, and saying unto him, Cornelius. And when he looked on him, he was afraid, and said, What is it, Lord? And he said unto him, Thy prayers and thine alms are come up for a memorial before God. (Acts 10:3-4)

Angels may Remain Invisible to the Naked Eye

Prophet Elisha saw angels of horses, chariots, and fire surrounding him yet his servant who was standing beside him did not perceive their presence. It was only after Elisha prayed that God would open his servants' eyes that his servant was able to see the heavenly host sent by God to defend them against their enemy:

And when the servant of the man of God was risen early, and gone forth, behold, an host compassed the city both with horses and chariots. And his servant said unto him, Alas, my master! how shall we do? And he answered, Fear not: for they that be with us are more than they that be with them. And Elisha prayed, and said, LORD, I pray thee, open his eyes, that he may see. And the LORD opened the eyes of the young man; and he saw: and, behold, the mountain was full of horses and chariots of fire round about Elisha. (2 Kings 6:15-17)

When the angel of the Lord appeared unto Daniel by the side of the great river, there were other men with him yet Daniel was the only man to see the angel:

Then I lifted up mine eyes, and looked, and behold a certain man clothed in linen, whose loins were girded with fine gold of Uphaz: His body also was like the beryl, and his face as the appearance of lightning, and his eyes as lamps of fire, and his arms and his feet like in colour to polished brass, and the voice of his words like the voice of a multitude. And I Daniel alone saw the vision: for the men that were with me saw not the vision; but a great quaking fell upon them, so that they fled to hide themselves. (Daniel 10:5-7)

Angels Can Be Discerned by Animals

When the angel of the Lord was sent to stand against Balaam, he did not discern the angel that was standing before him yet his horse saw the angel clearly.

> *And the ass saw the angel of the Lord standing in the way, and his sword drawn in his hand: and the ass turned aside out of the way, and went into the field: and Balaam smote the ass, to turn her into the way. But the angel of the Lord stood in a path of the vineyards, a wall being on this side, and a wall on that side. And when the ass saw the angel of the Lord, she thrust herself unto the wall, and crushed Balaam's foot against the wall: and he smote her again. And the angel of the Lord went further, and stood in a narrow place, where was no way to turn either to the right hand or to the left. And when the ass saw the angel of the Lord, she fell down under Balaam: and Balaam's anger was kindled, and he smote the ass with a staff. (Numbers 22:23-27)*

It was not until the Lord opened Balaam's eyes that he could see the angel in his way:

> *Then the Lord opened the eyes of Balaam, and he saw the angel of the Lord standing in the way, and his sword drawn in his hand: and he bowed down his head, and fell flat on his face.* (Numbers 22:31)

How many times have you witnessed animals around you acting out of character? Many times I have witnessed dogs barking and staring at something or hiding from fear of something that was not visible to my naked eyes. We must pay attention to animals. In Balaam's case, the horse's actions are what saved his life from destruction by the angel.

The natural man cannot discern the things of the spirit; they must be spiritually discerned (1 Corinthians 2:14). The closer we as believers enter into the spiritual realm, the more we will learn to discern the things of the spirit.

Prophet Elisha was a man who was used by God to perform great miracles, signs, and wonders. It is no wonder that he was one of the few people who did not fear angelic encounters and was able to see angels plainly when they were invisible to others around him.

Loosing God's Angels into Your Life

Loosing God's Angels into Your Life

When the disciples asked Jesus how they should pray Jesus directed them to pray that The Father's Kingdom would come and His will be done in the earth as it is in heaven (Matthew 6:10). God desires that His Kingdom come to the earth realm and the only way the Kingdom of God can come to Earth is through the lives of born again believers filled with His Spirit. God has given unto us free access to loose from His Kingdom to the earth realm anything we desire (Matthew 16:19).

> *"And I will give unto thee the keys of the kingdom of heaven: and whatsoever thou shalt bind on Earth shall be bound in heaven: and whatsoever thou shalt loose on Earth shall be loosed in heaven."* (Matthew 16:19)

As we unlock the doors of Gods' Kingdom we will encounter heaven's wealth. As we gain greater revelation of heaven's wealth we will have greater understanding of all that the Father desires to release upon His children in the earth realm. Anything that is within God's Kingdom is available to us through faith and we don't have to wait until we get to heaven to enjoy heaven's wealth. Today we can welcome and receive it in the earth realm.

To have been granted keys to a Kingdom or any place give us the means whereby we can open and close – loose and release –anything therein. We have been welcomed by God to access anything within His Kingdom. To have an owner or ruler to grant us this access implies a sense of trust, which requires relationship with the owner. Jesus voices this access to the Kingdom of God to Peter only after he (Peter) received the revelation from God of whom Jesus Christ was (Matthew 16:17).

> *And Jesus answered and said unto him, "Blessed art thou, Simon Barjona: for flesh and blood hath not revealed it unto thee, but my Father which is in heaven."* (Matthew 16:17)

Our access to the Kingdom of God will only be granted through our revelation of who Jesus Christ is and that will only come through relationship with our Heavenly Father. This relationship determines the degree that we fully access those things within His Kingdom.

Jesus said "no man cometh to the Father but by me" (John 14:6). The closer our relationship is with the heavenly Father the greater access we will have in His Kingdom; and those who truly know God will do exploits (Daniel 11:32).

By having the keys to God's Kingdom and the authority to loose and bind, we can release the angels to come to the earth realm. We only have to insert the key to unlock heavens doors and ask the Father to loose the angels to the earth.

I admonish you to understand that although we have been granted authority to loose angels to the earth through Christ, we do not have the authority over God's angels. God has granted us the power to unlock heaven and loose angels into the earth realm <u>through</u> Christ Jesus.

Angels are a part of God's Kingdom therefore we as born-again believers have the authority to use the keys given to us to open the Kingdom of God and loose the angels to work in the earth realm on our behalf. As we increase in our knowledge of Jesus Christ, God, and His Kingdom, we will learn how to unleash angels to move on our behalf, experience a greater revelation of angels and experience more angelic encounters in our lives.

As mentioned in an earlier section, angels are not under the control of man. They get their orders directly from God. We do not control the angels, although there are certain actions that we can take as a believer that will cause angels to be loosed from heaven on our behalf; they include:

1. Faith in God
2. Personal Relationship with God
3. Confessing the Word of God
4. Prayer
5. Crying out to God
6. Worshiping God

I
Angels are Loosed through our Faith

To unlock heaven's doors and loose anything therein we must first have faith in God. Without faith it is impossible to please God for those who come to Him and His Kingdom must first believe that He (and His Kingdom) is and that He rewards those who diligently seek Him (Hebrews 11:6). Just as everything else in the Kingdom of God, angels are activated through our faith.

God granting us the keys to heaven is of little benefit to us if we don't believe, for everything in the Kingdom of God is faith activated – even our Salvation:

But without faith it is impossible to please him: for he that cometh to God must believe that he is, and that he is a rewarder of them that diligently seek him. (Hebrews 11:6)

Angels are a part of God's Kingdom and our unbelief does not make them any less existent. Unbelief will only limit angelic activity in the life of the unbeliever.

God has released many spiritual gifts into the church yet all who believe in Christ do not accept or believe in every spiritual gift. For example, there are some believers who do not believe in the gift of prophecy – there are some that do. Those that do not believe in the gift of prophecy do not hinder its operation in the lives of those that do believe. However, due to their lack of faith, they bind the gift of prophecy in their own life and will not benefit from that particular gift.

I have noticed that church organizations that do not welcome the Holy Spirit into their midst do not experience any great moves of God. The Holy Spirit does not enter into hearts where He is not welcome.

God will not force us to receive any of His gifts. If we as believers want to experience the Kingdom of God in the earth realm and enjoy the full benefit of what heaven is offering then we must open our hearts to receive them through faith. We must welcome and release the angels of God to come and assist us.

If you bind the angels from working on your behalf in the earth, then God will not release them from the heavens. If you loose the angels to work for you in the earth realm then God will release them from the heavens to help you (Matthew 16:19, 18:18).

II
Angels are Loosed through our Relationship with God

When a sinner repents the angels are activated and begin to rejoice in heaven over the one who has given their life to God (Luke 10:15). Salvation grants us access to angels for they are sent by God to aid those who are to inherit salvation (Hebrews 1:14). When we receive Jesus Christ as our Lord and personal Savior we gain access to the Kingdom of God and all of its benefits including angelic assistance.

After receiving salvation we must then work to cultivate a personal relationship with God through His Son Jesus Christ. Any action we take that will move God will also move His angels. Receiving salvation grants us the access to heaven but the knowledge of His Kingdom and cultivating a personal relationship with Christ helps us to understand the benefits available to us as heirs.

As an employee, there are many benefits available to me. Last year, I noticed that the company I work for began offering tuition reimbursement to its' employees – this was a new benefit. After questioning one of our Human Resource representatives, she informed me that that the tuition reimbursement had been available for a while and that it was included in the benefits package.

I'd never taken the time to read through the updated benefits package; therefore, I was not aware of this and missed out on benefitting from this particular benefit. Though this benefit was available to all employees, I walked in ignorance concerning the availability of this benefit because I never read the book! The benefit was there – it was available to me but I failed to gain this knowledge.

It's the same in the Kingdom of God: we fail to experience the fullness of God's Kingdom in the earth realm because we lack knowledge of His promises. There are many spiritual gifts and benefits available to the believer, but if we fail to study the Word of God and become aware of what the Kingdom of God has to offer we will never experience the fullness of His Kingdom in the earth realm.

As children of the Most High God – He desires to grant unto us the desires of our heart. As a believer, to delight ourselves in the sight of God is to give our hearts to Him and live a life surrendered to His will.

Now by no means am I saying that only those who are in right standing with God will benefit from His angels. God reigns over the just as well as the unjust – He is gracious to us all. Yet when we live lives surrendered to God we experience more of heaven in the earth realm.

III
Angels are Loosed when we Confess the Word of God

God honors His Word. When we confess the Word of God in faith, He will send His angels to fulfill that which was spoken. Believers do not have to pray to God to ask for angelic assistance on those things that God has already promised. The angels are familiar with the spoken words of God. God does not change His mind concerning His promises.

He stood behind His word when they were initially spoken and He still stands behind them today, thousands of years later. The promises of God have no expiration date – God will forever stand behind His Word.

We activate angels when we speak the Word of God over our lives and the lives of our family. Psalms 103 contains an important Scripture to remember when it comes activating angels on our behalf:

> *Bless the Lord, ye his angels that excel in strength, that do his commandments, hearkening unto the voice of his word. Bless ye the Lord, all ye his hosts; ye ministers of his, that do his pleasure.* (vv. 20-21)

Angels are activated when the Word of God is spoken through faith. We are the voice of the Word of God. The Word goes out and the angels respond. When the Word of God is spoken through the lips of believers the angels of God take heed.

When believers speak the Word of God in faith it is as though an alarm sounds in the heavens and the angels of the Lord stand at attention to hear the Word of God to immediately fulfill it. The angels are not subject to us but when we speak the Word of God they hearken unto the voice that speaks His Word (Psalm 103:20-21).

When Daniel sought God for understanding, the angel responded, "Fear not, Daniel: for from the first day that thou didst set thine heart to understand and to chasten thyself before thy God, thy words were heard, and I am come for thy **words**" (Daniel 10:12, emphasis added).

Had Daniel never released his words up to God, the angels would never have come to help him. It is our responsibility to speak the Word of God whether in our prayers, songs, declarations, or confessions. When believers fail to speak the Word of God over their lives, they limit the miracle working power of God through the angels in that particular area. Many believers perish because of their lack of knowledge concerning the promises (Words) of God (Hosea 4:6).

To angels, the Word of God is similar to standard operating procedures used by employees for the daily operations of a business. Standard operating procedures have already received the stamp of approval from the authorizing agents. Employees do not need to seek direction or approval from authorizing agents on those matters that have been covered in the standard operating manual.

If you are not aware of the standard operating procedures of your job then you will fail as an employee. It works the same way in the spirit realm. If you do not know the Word of God and His promises concerning your life, you will fail in life and live beneath God's plan for you.

The Word of God has already been approved by God and is forever established in the heavens (Psalm 119:89). Angels already have the approval of God to act when the words of God are spoken. Angels are aware of their responsibility to fulfill God's words when we speak them, they don't have to wait for God to approve it a second time.

Just as our speaking Gods words and promises over our life releases His angels to work on our behalf, speaking in opposition to God's promises cause us not to receive the fullness of God's promises. Angels cannot assist us when we allow negative words and negative confessions to be released from our mouth. Negative words stop the miracle working power of God and stop the work of the angels.

Angels of God are standing by His throne awaiting your release of His word and promises from your lips. When we decree and declare the Word of God over our lives, angels go into action to fulfill that word. They are ready to step into action and change situations on our behalf. Have faith to know that when you speak God's word in faith, the angels get to work immediately to accomplish that which was spoken.

IV
Angels are Loosed when we Pray

Angels are activated when the believer prays. Father God yearns to communicate with His children and it brings the Father joy to grant us the desires of our heart. When we make our desires known unto God and they align with the Word of God, His angels move swiftly into action to fulfill His promises.

Our prayers activate the angels to fulfill the spoken Word of God over our lives. The angels of God are encamped around the believer and around the throne of God. When believers pray to God – angels of God collect those prayers to present them to God. Revelation 8:4 tells us that the prayers of the saints ascended up before God out of the angel's hand as the smoke from incense.

As mentioned earlier, we are not to pray to angels. We pray to God and He will send His angels to answer our prayers. The sincere prayers of the righteous availeth much (James 5:16). Our prayers touch the heart of God. When the heart of God is touched, the angels of God are activated. In both the Old and New Testament, angels were sent by God to answer the prayers of the saints.

God Sent an Angel to Answer Zacharias' Prayers

In Luke 1, while a multitude of people were outside the temple praying, Zacharias was in the temple burning incense and praying before the altar of the Lord. While prayers were going up before God, an angel of the Lord appeared on the right side of the altar causing fear to fall upon Zacharias. The angel informs Zacharias, *"Fear not, Zacharias: for thy prayer is heard; and thy wife Elisabeth shall bear thee a son, and thou shalt call his name John."* (Luke 1:13)

As the multitude of prayers was going up before the Lord, the angel of the Lord arrived on the scene and responded to fulfill their request. Angels respond in this very manner today when the prayers of believers are sent up before God. We learn in Revelation that our prayers rise up before God as incense:

> *And when he had taken the book, the four beasts and four and twenty elders fell down before the Lamb, having every one of them harps, and golden vials full of odours, which are the prayers of saints. (v. 5:8)*

God Sent an Angel to Answer the Saint's Prayers for Peter

In Acts 12, Herod had imprisoned Peter because of his faith. Not only does Herod imprison Peter, he goes further and orders that he be bound with two chains, and instructs two soldiers to be assigned to his side. The keeper of the prison was to ensure that he did not escape.

This well thought out plan, devised by Herod, did not hinder the angels of God from rescuing Peter. While Peter was in prison, the church continued to send up prayers to God on his behalf. While the church was praying, God heard their prayers and sent an angel into the prison to personally escort Peter to freedom:

> *Peter therefore was kept in prison: but prayer was made without ceasing of the church unto God for him. And when Herod would have brought him forth, the same night Peter was sleeping between two soldiers, bound with two chains: and the keepers before the door kept the prison. And, behold, the angel of the Lord came upon him, and a light shined in the prison: and he smote Peter on the side, and raised him up, saying, Arise up quickly. And his chains fell off from his hands. And the angel said unto him, Gird thyself, and bind on thy sandals. And so he did. And he saith unto him, Cast thy garment about thee, and follow me. And he went out, and followed him; and wist not that it was true which was done by the angel; but thought he saw a vision. When they were past the first and the second ward, they came unto the Iron*

gate that leadeth unto the city; which opened to them of his own accord: and they went out, and passed on through one street; and forthwith the angel departed from him. And when Peter was come to himself, he said, Now I know of a surety, that the Lord hath sent his angel, and hath delivered me out of the hand of Herod, and from all the expectation of the people of the Jews. (Acts 12:5-11)

God Sent an Angel to Answer Daniel's Prayers

Daniel set his face toward the Lord to make requests by prayer and supplications with fasting sackcloth and ashes (Daniel 9:3). As Daniel was speaking in prayer before the Lord, the angel Gabriel was sent by God and informs Daniel:

O Daniel, I am now come forth to give thee skill and understanding. At the beginning of thy supplications the commandment came forth, and I am come to shew thee; for thou art greatly beloved: therefore understand the matter, and consider the vision. (Daniel 9:22-23)

Note that the angel Gabriel was given the command to go to Daniel at the beginning of his prayers when he first sought understanding from God. We must understand that God responds immediately to our prayers just as He did for Daniel. Our heavenly Father desires to answer the prayers of His children and as believers we must know that our prayers to God are not in vain. As we pray to God, He sends forth His commandments upon the earth and the angels run swiftly to perform His words.

Just as our prayers activate angels, our lack of praying binds them from moving on our behalf. What would the outcome of Elisabeth and Zacchaeus's desire for a son have been had they never taken their request to God in prayer? Would Peter have died in prison had the church not continuously lifted him to God in prayer? Would Daniel have received the revelation he sought?

Many believers today suffer lack and lead defeated Christian lives because they fail to pray. Their lives have become so busy and their reliance is so on their own abilities that they no longer fit praying to God in their daily routine. Our nation is in turmoil, our communities are flooded with ungodliness, and our families suffer lack (spiritually and naturally) because we fail to seek God in prayer.

If Zacharias and Elisabeth's prayers to God led to the conception of John the Baptist, the saints' prayers for Peter led to his freedom from prison, and Daniels' prayers brought an angel of revelation— what will your prayers to God do for you? In what areas of your life do you need God to release angelic assistance?

As a child of God, your sincere prayer to God will activate the angels and change your situation. Our prayers set angels into action.

V
Angels are Loosed when We Cry Out to God

Our Father in heaven is alert to the sound of the cries from His children. When our cries reach the ear of God, it touches His heart and He can send angels to our aid. We see this in Jeremiah 33:3, "Call unto me, and I will answer thee, and show thee great and mighty things, which thou knowest not".

Hezekiah Cried Out to God

After being threatened by King Sennacherib of Assyria; Hezekiah and the prophet Isaiah prayed and cried out to heaven – in response God sent an angel to their aid:

> *Now because of this King Hezekiah and the prophet Isaiah, the son of Amoz, prayed and cried out to heaven. Then the Lord sent an angel who cut down every mighty man of valor, leader, and captain in the camp of the king of Assyria. So he returned shamefaced to his own land. And when he had gone into the temple of his god, some of his own offspring struck him down with the sword there. Thus the Lord saved Hezekiah and the inhabitants of Jerusalem from the hand of Sennacherib the king of Assyria, and from the hand of all others, and guided them on every side. (2 Chronicles 32:20-22)*

Hagar Wept

After being sent away by Abraham, Hagar wept and an angel of the Lord was sent in response to her son's voice:

> *And she went, and sat her down over against him a good way off, as it were a bow shot: for she said, Let me not see the death of the child. And she sat over against him, and lift up her voice, and wept. And God heard the voice of the lad; and the angel of God called to Hagar out of heaven, and said unto her, What aileth thee, Hagar? fear not; for God hath heard the voice of the lad where he is.* (Genesis 21:16-17)

The Children of Israel Cried Out to the Lord

God sent an angel to rescue the children of Israel out of the hands of the Egyptians after they cried out to Him:

> *And when we cried unto the LORD, he heard our voice, and sent an angel, and hath brought us forth out of Egypt: and, behold, we are in Kadesh, a city in the uttermost of thy border.* (Numbers 20:16)

In whatever areas of our lives we find ourselves in need, we must believe that the angels of God are always available. You may be in a situation where you feel like giving up, facing great loss in your life, or not know if you can go any further. Wherever you are, there are innumerable angels standing before God awaiting your cries to Him for help and His directive to them to go and aid you.

God's desire is that we, His children cry out to Him in our time of need. God hears the cries of the righteous and delivers them out of all their troubles (Psalm 34:17).

VI
Angels are Loosed when We Worship God

Angels are activated in atmospheres where God is worshipped. Whether you are worshiping the Lord with a group or alone, listening to worship music or singing praises all by yourself, angels are activated. Angels love to worship God and they are drawn to those atmospheres where worship is occurring so that they too can participate.

The seraphim were described as being positioned above the throne of God. Their closeness to God is directly related to their role, which is that of continuously worshiping God and ushering in His glory:

> *And one cried unto another, and said, Holy, holy, holy, is the Lord of hosts: the whole earth is full of his glory. And the posts of the door moved at the voice of him that cried, and the house was filled with smoke.* (Isaiah 6:3-4)

The purpose of our worship is to glorify, honor, praise, exalt, and please God. Our worship is a display of our adoration and loyalty to God for His saving grace towards us. That God would assign those angels with the closest proximity to Him the responsibility of constantly worshiping helps us to have a greater revelation of the effect that our offering of praise and worship has on God. Worship grants us closeness to our God spiritually, and as we draw closer to Him – He draws closer to us (James 4:8).

Personally, I have never felt closer to God then when I am offering up the sacrifice of my praise and worship to Him. I have been a part worship services when God was being adored, honored, and worshipped in which people have proclaimed to see angels of God flying around in the building or they themselves being brushed by angel wings.

God is enthroned in our worship (Psalm 22:3) because our worship exalts Him as our personal God and Savior. In whatever place God is enthroned, the seraphim are present standing above His throne and ushering in His glory. Having the presence of angels in your midst is a sure sign that God is present.

Angels Gather in Atmospheres Where God is Worshipped

As a worship leader, there are too many occasions for me to try to count where it was clear that angelic activity was at work. Most have been audible sounds of unseen voices helping me sing and fill the atmosphere in song. Many such occasions have occurred during my devotional times either at home or in our mission base's prayer room, where perhaps only a few were gathered.

I remember playing the piano one "night-watch" in the prayer room, singing a song, and hearing perfect harmony with every note that I sung. In fact, even the sound of the piano changed to something divine. I actually stopped for several moments, looking around the room to see if anyone else was singing, but the real problem was that I was singing a spontaneous song that God was birthing in that very moment, so of course no other person (human) could be singing in sync with me. I continued singing and continued to hear perfect harmonies with my words and melodies. It was quite awesome!

In another worship service, I had an open vision of two huge angels coming down into the building. But these were not human in size by any means; they were at least 50 feet tall and muscular. The one closest to me knelt down near the stage but as if he was kneeling on another unseen platform. He had a long white robe with what looked like a white flowing cape on his back, a dull skin complexion, but purple light glowing both around and on him. He took out a bow and began to shoot arrows all throughout the building. The other angel was a little smaller and was very active behind the large angel, but I could not see what he was doing. It was so real that I momentarily wondered why no one else could see this.

Prophet Nathan Irving
Intercessory Missionary
Frederick Maryland

Conclusion

Angels are in Partnership with You to Fulfill Your Destiny

Jacob, after having received his father's instruction and blessing, embarks on a journey fleeing from his brother Esau whom he learned desires to kill him. On his way to Haran he stops to rest and has a dream as recorded in Genesis 28:10-22 in which he sees a ladder or stairway reaching from Earth to heaven. He sees angels of God ascending and descending, with the Lord standing above the stairway proclaiming to Jacob who He is, and what He promises to do for him.

When Jacob awakes, he says, "Surely the Lord is in this place and I was not aware of it. How awesome is this place! This is none other than the house of God; this is the gate of heaven" (Genesis 28:16-17, NIV). The next morning he calls the place Bethel, meaning house of God (v. 19).

Can you imagine what this dream did for Jacob's faith and confidence in his time of anxiety? It's a powerful revelation Jacob receives: that God was with him even in his time of fear, as he was on the run from Esau's murderous intentions.

It's interesting that in the dream the angels are first ascending to God in heaven before descending back down to Earth. That means they were already just waiting for him to get there. Isn't it amazing how God has given us such an elevated place of partnership with Him as we are called to be involved with His plans and purpose in the earth?

Our destinies are so important and strategically linked to God's plan for each generation that they actually include an open heaven gateway for angelic intervention. They are watching over our lives and destinies and ascending to heaven for instructions, and descending back down with answers and strategies.

Brenda K. Fields

*Father – open our eyes
to see this incredible invisible gateway to heaven,
and the multitudes of angels ready to act on our behalf.
Thank you for your Word that is life and spirit
and for your Rhema word that causes faith to come.
In Jesus name!*

**Apostle Axel Sippach
Founder EPIC Global Network**

God wants to establish His Kingdom here on Earth and His Kingdom will only come through the surrendered lives of Spirit-filled believers who are ready to go to the next level in Christ. The more we enter into the Spirit realm through worship and developing an intimate relationship with our Heavenly Father, the more open our spirits become to entertain and discern angels without fear.

It is very important that as children of the Living God we consistently seek His face and His heart, and inquire as to the directions we should take. Don't lose hope in these last days but remember that there are innumerable angels standing around the throne of God awaiting an opportunity to come to our aid and assigned by God to keep us in all of our ways (Psalm 91:11).

As born-again believers, we have been given the keys to the Kingdom of God. We hold the keys to unleashing angels upon the earth to work on our behalf (Matthew 18:18-19). My prayer is that through your study of this book you have *Awaken to Angels*.

About the Author

Brenda Fields has been gifted by God to serve in many roles within the body of Christ. She is an Author, Teacher, Administrator, Organizer, and Mentor.

As a Five Fold Ministry Teacher, Brenda has a passion to see the Word of God taught with accuracy and simplicity so it can be understood and applied to the lives of Spirit-filled believers. Her teachings challenge believers to go to the next level in their faith by believing and stepping into the promises of God. She has taught on such topics as Understanding Spiritual Gifts, Understanding Dreams and Visions, Using your Spiritual Gifts as Evangelistic Tools, and Increasing Your Faith.

Outside of the church, Ms. Fields has served as a Manager of Performance / Quality Improvement for more than 15 years. She combines her experience in organizational development and performance improvement to assist churches in developing structure and restoring order so they can achieve their God-given missions. Her goal is to see the church function as a healthy body, fitly joined together and growing.

Ms. Fields is a graduate of Wallace College in Selma Alabama and Alabama State University, where she earned an Associate's in Nursing and a Bachelor's in Health Information Management, respectively.

For information on booking or to contact the Author:
Email: AuthorBrendaFields@gmail.com
Fax: 1-866-823-5529
Facebook: Author Brenda Fields

Other Books by Author Brenda Fields

Keys to Becoming Victorious Women
"Lessons Learned from Women of the Bible"

The Word of God provides us with master keys to unlock doors of victory in every area of our life. In *Keys to Becoming a Victorious Woman,* Fields discusses 26 biblical keys demonstrated by women of the bible that led them to monumental victories that left their mark in bible history. When applied today, these 26 keys will unlock doors to your next level of victory spiritually, professionally and relationally. You can experience this same power as victorious women of the bible by studying each section, adopting the characteristics you will learn about in each lesson, and walking through the doors you will unlock as you progress on your journey toward victory. **You are called to be a victorious woman – are you ready to become one?**

ISBN 978-1-942814-00-9

References

The following versions of The Holy Bible were used within the pages of this book. King James, New King James Version and New International Version.

(KJV) King James Version, Publisher: Public Domain

(NKJV) Scripture taken from the New King James Version®. Copyright © 1982 by Thomas Nelson. Used by permission. All rights reserved.

(NIV) THE HOLY BIBLE, NEW INTERNATIONAL VERSION®, NIV® Copyright © 1973, 1978, 1984, 2011 by Biblica, Inc.® Used by permission. All rights reserved worldwide.

Enoch, E. (2016, January 30). Story of Mr. John Birchfield, *"The Sharecropper's son who built billion-dollar enterprises returning to Tuscaloosa after 85 years"*. In *The Tuscaloosa News*. (Reprinted with Permission)

Multiple words. 2016. In *Merriam-Webster.com*. Retrieved August 20, 2016, from https://www.merriam-webster.com/dictionary

Strong, J., & Strong, J. (1984). *The New Strong's exhaustive concordance of the Bible: With main concordance, appendix to the main concordance, key verse comparison chart, dictionary of the Hebrew Bible, dictionary of the Greek Testament*. Nashville: Thomas Nelson Publishers.

Thayer & Smith. (1999). In *Greek Lexicon entry for Angel. The NAS New Testament Greek Lexicon.* Retrieved at http://www.biblestudytools.com/lexicons/greek/nas/

In Thomas, R. L. (1981). *New American standard exhaustive concordance of the Bible: Including Hebrew-Aramaic and Greek dictionaries.*

M.G. Easton M.A., D.D. (1897), Illustrated Bible Dictionary, Third Edition, published by Thomas Nelson, 1897. Retrieved at http://www.biblestudytools.com/dictionary

Notes

Notes

www.ingramcontent.com/pod-product-compliance
Lightning Source LLC
Chambersburg PA
CBHW071520080526
44588CB00011B/1506